"It was something
and softly, fading in
a

THE SOUND
of
FLEETWOOD MAC

had taken a decade to develop and the talents of twelve people over the years to define. Now it has taken the music world by storm.

Here in this authorized history, discover how the sound was shaped and how Fleetwood Mac solidified into its present group: Mick Fleetwood (drums), and John McVie (bass), Christine Perfect McVie (keyboard, vocal), Lindsey Buckingham (guitar, vocal) and Stephanie "Stevie" Nicks (vocal and guitar). Learn about the members who came and left: Jeremy Spencer, with his talent for parody, and his strange disappearance; Danny Kirwan, whose unique guitar style featured "vibrato in the fingerwork" and whose problem personality lost him his place; Peter Green, with his hard rock influence on the group, and the influence of other people's troubles upon him. Find out what the group thinks will happen to them in the wake of the much publicized Buckingham-Nicks and McVie-McVie splits. Look ahead with Fleetwood Mac as the group moves on past "Rumours" into the solid platinum future...

THE AUTHORIZED HISTORY

FLEETWOOD MAC

BY SAMUEL GRAHAM

WARNER BOOKS

A Warner Communications Company

Warner Books are
distributed in the
United Kingdom by

NEW ENGLISH LIBRARY

WARNER BOOKS EDITION

ISBN 0-446-89984-4

Warner Books, Inc., 75 Rockefeller Plaza, New York, N.Y. 10019

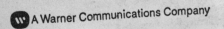 A Warner Communications Company

Printed in the United States of America

Not associated with Warner Press, Inc., of Anderson, Indiana

First Printing: November, 1978

10 9 8 7 6 5 4 3

ACKNOWLEDGEMENTS: THE AUTHOR'S grateful thanks to Judy Wong, without whom this project might never have been completed, and to Jim Bickhart, who helped get it off the ground. Thanks also to the following, who either helped arrange interviews or submitted to them themselves: Sharon Weisz, Gabriele Arras, Mike Vernon, Clifford Davis, Harvey Schaps, Andy Mitchell, Don Schmitzerle, Mickey Shapiro, *Record World* magazine, and of course, members of Fleetwood Mac, past and present (Peter Green, Mick Fleetwood, John McVie, Christine McVie, Bob Welch, Stevie Nicks and Lindsey Buckingham).

Fleetwood Mac 1978. (l. to r.) Christine McVie, Mick Fleetwood, Lindsey Buckingham, John McVie, Stevie Nicks.

INTRODUCTION

TOWARDS THE END OF 1975, SOMETHING good happened to the nation's AM radio playlists. It came on smoothly and softly, groping its way through the static on your tiny car speaker, fading in on a thick bed of electric organ and acoustic guitar, colored with lightly picked harmonics. You relaxed and let a few more miles drift by, as a sultry alto sang:

> You can take me to paradise
> then again you can be cold as ice
> I'm Over My Head,
> But it sure feels nice.

And it did feel nice. Later, somewhere between the disco McDonald's commercials and the earnest appeals from smarmy salesmen, the disc jockey unhinged his jaw from 8000 rpm's long enough to identify the song as " 'Over My Head,' and that's the super solid sayin' somethin' sounds of Fleetwood Mac!" Fleetwood Mac, eh?...Seems to me I've heard of them somewhere...They've been around a while, haven't they?

They've been around, all right. Over ten years. After being formed in 1967 out of mutual devotion to the blues, Fleetwood Mac rode the crest of the British "blues boom" into rock stardom, producing a string of devastating hit singles in England. But they failed to significantly crack the American market until much later, when suddenly, after treading for years just on the safer side of obscurity here, Fleetwood Mac erupted. "Over My Head" began a surge by this veteran band that has culminated in their being the top rock attraction in the U.S., and very likely the world as well, as this is written.

After "Over My Head" came "Rhiannon," a major hit, and then "Say You Love Me." Sales of *Fleetwood Mac*, the album from which they were all culled, reached "gold," then "platinum," then multiple-platinum status, running well over four million copies. And if there was ever much debate as to the Mac's ability to make a strong follow-up, the stylish *Rumours* quickly stifled it. Like its predecessor, *Rumours* was a triumph of accessibility. As sales have reached stratospheric levels and radio airplay on both AM and FM stations continues unabated, it has proved itself both qualitatively and quantitatively durable.

Hand in hand with the sales came the accolades. Starting with the 1976 Don Kirshner Rock Awards, Fleetwood Mac swept nearly every "best group" and "best album" award (and variations of same) that was handed out through magazines, television presentations, polls and so on. The '77 Kirshner Awards, the American Music Awards, the *Crawdaddy* Awards, the top spots in the *Rolling Stone* critic and reader polls, and a '77 Grammy: these comprise only a few of the kudos lavished on Fleetwood Mac.

Moreover, they found themselves coping with the business of being celebrities. Sensuous singer Stevie Nicks became the new rock 'n' roll *femme fatale*, her love life the subject of countless inane rumors (the album title of the same name was, of course, no coincidence). The whole band was featured in a *People* magazine cover story, certainly an indication of notoriety extending beyond the rock milieu, while *Rolling Stone's* Random Notes and other gossip-oriented oracles reported at length on every development in their (at one point) rather tangled personal lives. No question about it, Fleetwood Mac established a firm foothold among rock's aristocracy.

Besides Stevie Nicks (age 29), Fleetwood Mac now consists of drummer Mick Fleetwood (30), the group's practical main man, bass guitarist John McVie (31), the free spirit, Christine McVie (33), the relaxed and straightforward keyboardist, and guitarist Lindsey Buckingham (28), the unassuming, dedicated musical leader. Through all of their success, this quintet has managed to keep its collective feet planted firmly on the ground. They are naturally enjoying the fruits of popularity, yet they hardly fit the rock star image. No huge sycophantic entourages, no hotel demolitions, no drunken public scenes. The attention focused on their personal doings has hardly been encouraged by the band; while it may be true that Stevie (and to some extent the others as well) spends a certain amount of time in the papers, it isn't necessarily by choice. They are not royalty, they are working musicians.

While the band has had a fairly solid base of support for some years, it's safe to say that a vast portion of their audience is unaware of Fleetwood Mac's long history. The current line-up has now been together for about three years, and *Rumours* marks only the third time in some dozen releases (excluding various compilations and reissues) that the same personnel has made two consecutive lps. Twelve members have been involved in eight or nine different line-ups; only Fleetwood and John McVie have appeared on every album.

The numerous personnel shifts certainly haven't been much help to the cause of an ongoing identity. But Fleetwood Mac has a tradition. There have been periods in its evolution bearing little resemblance to other periods, but some intuitive, undefined persona has endured. It's in the styles of the various guitarists, the vocalists, the songs and attitudes each new member has brought in, or the redoubtable Fleet-wood-McVie rhythm section. Each has contributed to what Mick Fleetwood aptly calls "a simple, honest approach to music." And as this remarkable band begins its second decade, many of us would argue that their success is long overdue.

CHAPTER 1

I N THE SIMPLEST POSSIBLE TERMS, THE ROLES
of England and America in the development of
rock music can be clearly separated: the Americans "invented" it, the English imported and refined
it. This is a vital distinction, and one that's central to
each country's perception of the music that has
dominated both sides of the Atlantic for the last
twenty years.

It was in the U.S. that Elvis Presley, Little Richard,
Chuck Berry and their peers crisscrossed and consolidated various traditions—blues, rhythm and
blues, folk, country, jazz—into rock and roll. Young
American musicians who played rock assimilated
these traditions naturally, subconsciously. This was
the music they had always heard on their radios, or in
the dance halls of their towns and bars of their cities;
they had grown up with it, and rock was simply the
end result of that growth.

The English, on the other hand, were acutely aware that rock music was not indigenous to their country. While Americans were effortlessly absorbing their past, Britishers were studying it, paying tribute to it and constantly developing it.

By the time of the mid-60s "British invasion," artists like Buddy Holly, Carl Perkins, Chuck Berry and Muddy Waters had already made an impact on American music. But every English band that reached our promised land, as well as countless others who dwelled in near obscurity in England, played at least a few numbers by the masters. Even those who soon pioneered new forms were quick to acknowledge their debt to the origins of the music. And they took those origins *very* seriously.

Especially the blues. Oh, those Limeys and their blues. There was something in the experience of the black bluesman, whether a young and shiny-suited type or an old, weather-beaten rural singer, that perfectly stroked the imaginations of the white middle- and lower-class Englishmen. It was a basis for identification, perhaps a feeling of shared suffering, that went much deeper than the music alone.

Long after the Beatles had made rock an "important" form, the blues movement remained a formidable part of the British scene. When the staunchest early blues and R&B proponents had moved on (and the best white American blues band, Paul Butterfield's, had expanded its strict format) English groups like Chicken Shack, Savoy Brown and others were still staking their musical lives on the blues. Later, a whole new generation of groups (typified by Free, the Climax Blues Band or Led Zeppelin) began their careers playing lots of blues. "The Blues Boom" was a bona fide phenomenon.

ONE MAN WHO PLAYED AN ACTIVE ROLE IN making it so was Mike Vernon, an engineer and eventually staff producer at Decca Records' studio in West Hampstead, London. Vernon had gotten a taste of American blues during grammar school, and he nurtured a passion for it, everything from Son House to Robert Johnson to Bo Diddley and Muddy Waters. He later started a publication called "R&B Monthly" with his brother Richard and Neil Slaven, another eventual Decca producer. They often went to London's Crawdaddy Club and Star Hotel to hawk the magazine and listen to the Yardbirds, at the time (mid-60s) the leading blues crusaders; on occasion Vernon would even sit in with the band when singer Keith Relf had one of his frequent attacks of laryngitis.

Vernon went on to Decca, where he was able to control his vicarious fantasies by producing young English blues bands (including Ten Years After and Savoy Brown) as well as a few visiting Americans. It was also at Decca that he and Gus Dudgeon (later Elton John's producer) worked with a musician who really gave English blues an injection: John Mayall, whose various bands were the proving ground for many a pop-star to be.

Mayall, it is now widely assumed, begat Eric Clapton, who sprang from John's fevered brow with distortion boosted and finger vibrato wailing. And it's true that even though he had been with the Yardbirds, Clapton's stint with Mayall's Bluesbreakers was his first big move, the era when he defined rock guitar even while playing blues. With Clapton, Mayall put British blues on the map.

Clapton went on to Cream, leaving behind the

Mike Vernon

hugely successful *Bluesbreakers* LP. His replacement with Mayall was Peter Green, and though he was never an international hero of Clapton's stature, Green became the new cynosure of the 60's blues cult. He epitomized real *blues* guitar and singing, English style, and he would make an even more profound local impression than his predecessor.

ONE OF THREE SONS OF A POOR JEWISH family in London's east end, Peter Green had first been taken with the guitar at age eleven, during what he calls "the skiffle days." One of his brothers brought home a cheap little Spanish guitar, which eventually became Peter's hand-me-down; "My brother showed me a few chords," he says, "and I took off."

Hank B. Marvin, a member of the instrumental group the Shadows, is not a man that many American guitarists would name in their individual litanies of the greats. But for young English players, including Clapton, Peter Frampton and plenty more, Hank Marvin was the reason they first picked up a guitar in earnest. So it was with Peter Green, who vividly remembers his brothers' supplying him with a cardboard model of Marvin's guitar.

Green's first exposure to the blues, he recalls, came from some old Muddy Waters 78's hoarded by one of Green's musician friends; that was "the first blues I consciously heard." Oddly enough, one of the guitarists who was later to be suggested as a prime influence, B.B. King, "didn't make any impression on me when I first heard him," Green says. And while he grew to admire B.B., and also Buddy Guy and Freddie King ("He was very simple—what I'd call brutally blues"), it was none other than Eric Clapton who inspired him to "make it" as a guitarist. "I was playing bass semi-professionally. But Clapton gave me a big boost to play lead guitar again. I thought, 'Maybe I can do that too,' after hearing him. He was the first big direction I had. I even got a Les Paul guitar because he played one."

Those old Muddy Waters sides had made their impression on Peter Green—"the whole thing sounded very spare, and very together"—and he became one of the few English bluesmen to effectively translate his subconscious affinity for the American form into an identity of his own. "My feel was mine alone," he now contends, "because I don't think you can recreate a feel. But when you're Jewish, you can still create a lot of feel of your own. I was always a very sad person—I don't really know why—and I suppose I felt a very deep sadness with my heritage. The blues was a natural outlet. But it was never the be-all and end-all for me."

Green eventually became a member of Peter B's (Bardens, now with Camel) Looners, playing Shadows, Booker T and the MGs and some blues; in that band he first played with a drummer named Mick Fleetwood (Fleetwood had also played earlier with Bardens, in the Cheynes). The Looners amalgamated into the Shotgun Express, which also included Rod Stewart and lesser luminaries like bassist Dave Ambrose and Beryl Marsden, a Liverpool singer. While Green "always swore I wouldn't take a job with John Mayall—I thought he didn't pay well enough," an unhappy love affair with Beryl Marsden made him want to leave Shotgun, and he accepted a gig with Mayall "as a bit of a challenge. I was very naive. I didn't understand the prestige of playing with Mayall, or the pressure of replacing Eric Clapton,

16

and I didn't care about it. I just enjoyed the chance to play the way I wanted."

MIKE VERNON: "IT WAS SOME TIME AFTER making the Clapton album before we got into the studio again, and when John Mayall turned up, he presented us with the news that Eric wasn't in the band anymore. Then he glibly announced that he'd found a new guitar player called Peter Green. When Green arrived with his guitar, he wore one of those Canadian-style checked lumber jackets and the usual format of blue jeans and plimsolls. He was very quiet and well mannered, rather insignificant, really. It wasn't until he started to play that Gus and I realized that he was an enormous talent, one that would need perhaps a little edging on but one that could certainly stand up against Eric, which was the unenviable position he found himself in."

Mayall's bassist was John McVie, who had gotten his start as a pro with the Bluesbreakers and had played on the Clapton album. Vernon recalls that McVie "had at that time quite a heavy drinking problem, which created a few hassles within the band. But it was a problem he seemed to manage to handle when it was really necessary. Mayall knew of his talents as a bass player, and he wasn't about to remove him from the outfit." With drummer Aynsley Dunbar, Mayall, Green and McVie recorded *A Hard Road*, a worthy successor to the Clapton sides that featured Green's work on a fiery instrumental called "The Supernatural."

Later on, when Mayall was at one point drummerless, Green suggested hiring Mick Fleetwood. Fleetwood admits he was surprised at being asked to join: "It was odd, because it was the one time I'd stopped playing drums professionally. I'd just started a little window cleaning business, but Pete just phoned me up out of the blue." His tenure with Mayall was short; he remembers it as five weeks, while Vernon says it was a mere twelve days. "I didn't have a drinking problem when I joined," Fleetwood recalls, "but I may have by the time I was fired. I got to know John, who was fairly well known for his alcohol intake—he'd been fired and rehired by Mayall three times or so." Yet while Fleetwood's own Mayall stint was brief, he impressed Mike Vernon as being "very solid and straightforward, probably the straightest drummer Mayall ever had. He was certainly less flairy than Aynsley."

GREEN, EVEN THOUGH GIVEN MORE OF the limelight than Mayall's other sidemen, eventually felt the constraints of the Blues-breakers, especially after he, McVie and Fleetwood (or possibly Dunbar, according to Mike Vernon) recorded a couple of tracks as a trio. "That was really the start of it, I think," says Vernon, "when Peter got a taste of being out in front of it all."

The nucleus of what was to be Fleetwood Mac thus had come together by way of the Mayall partnership. The name, rather obviously, came from Fleetwood and McVie. Unusual, perhaps, naming a band after its rhythm section, but "Pete was very preoccupied with not becoming a superstar guitarist, which he could easily have been," Fleetwood explains. "He wanted to downplay his own role."

Green felt that the trio would need another guitarist, one with a style cut from a different cloth than his own, and it was Mike Vernon who came up with the

18

right suggestion: "In those days I went around the country and saw a lot of bands for Decca, sort of talent hunts. I had a letter from this character Jeremy Spencer, who waffled on continually about Elmore James and Homesick James Williamson and would I come see his band, which was called the Levi Set Blues Group. So I went to hear them in a very small church on the outskirts of Litchfield—it was winter, and very cold. They were just a trio, and the bass player and drummer were very untight and really rather laughable. But Jeremy really blew me away. He was on the short side, with a flock of curly hair, not unlike Peter's, and he played slide on this large, F-hole semi-acoustic with a pick up. He was playing Elmore James songs—he even sang like Elmore James."

"I brought Jeremy's group to London and we did an audition one afternoon. With that rhythm section, it was catastrophic. Jeremy was totally convinced that they were the right musicians for him to work with, but Gus and I were rather loath to even offer the demo to Decca." What Vernon did do, however, was put Spencer together with Green. "The meeting between Peter and Jeremy came about as a direct result of my writing Jeremy and telling him that Peter was thinking of forming his own band," recalls Vernon. "I told Jeremy he should come hear John Mayall in Birmingham."

A S IT TURNED OUT, JOHN McVIE WAS TEM-porarily a little reluctant to leave Mayall, given the security offered by a steady gig. So Green and Fleetwood recruited Bob Brunning, a sometime teacher who "knew he was only tempo-rary," Fleetwood says. "He was quite flattered he'd been asked to join at all, because we were fairly well known on the club circuit after Mayall, especially Peter." And anyway, adds Green, "Bob Brunning wasn't really adequate. All he did was look at girls' tits all night when we played."

When McVie did leave Mayall, he felt some of the same discontent that had affected Peter Green. "I thought that Mayall was getting too jazzy, after he brought about three horns in," McVie told *Record World* magazine. "We were doing a gig in Norwich, and we did a sound check, working some arrangement out—this was when I was still a very hard-core blues addict, with the 'There is nothing outside of the blues' attitude. So one of the horn players asked, 'What kind of solo do you want in this section?' And I'll always remember, John said, 'Oh, just play free-form.' I thought to myself, 'OK, that's it.' We used to do two sets, so during the interval I went out and phoned up Greenie and said, 'Hey, you need a bass player?' "

Fleetwood Mac made its first appearance at the Windsor Jazz and Blues Festival on August 12, 1967. When the time came to record, they went with a young label, Mike Vernon's Blue Horizon Records. Blue Horizon had been a limited-edition operation for about a year, releasing a popular Mayall/Clapton single called "Lonely Years" and a few other blues tracks. "When Peter started talking about perhaps forming his own band," Vernon says, "he talked to me about the possibilities of getting Blue Horizon on the map at the same time as his prospective band. It seemed like a good idea, and the ideal time to do it. That's how Blue Horizon took a big step forward into being a major label."

The first single, recorded with Brunning, was "Believe

First Fleetwood Mac appearance '67–early '68 (l. to r.) John McVie, Mick Fleetwood (in back), Jeremy Spencer, Peter Green.

My Time Ain't Long," backed with "Rambling Pony." The A side was the first in a long line of Jeremy Spencer's Elmore James tributes. While Peter Green says that "Jeremy had his own feel, too," Spencer certainly came close to outright copies of his idol's patented licks, and he made no bones about it. His re-creations, this one adopted from the Robert Johnson standard "Dust My Broom," were generally very faithful. Only later, after six or eight of them appeared on the first couple of albums, did they threaten to become tiresome.

Spencer had five more slide numbers on the Mike Vernon-produced first album, and he again showed that his workouts were entertaining for their good naturedness as well as their authenticity. They were likable, if unconscious, caricatures; his macho singing, coming from this little white kid, was especially silly, but one felt that one was laughing *with* him, at least in part. At his worst ("Cold Black Night"), he was plodding and ponderous, leading a band that sounded like Lead Weight and the Cement Mixers. But at his best he had real energy and feeling, throwing himself into James' classic "Shake Your Moneymaker" and making it *swing*.

Green emerged as a serious and accomplished musician. He showed a mastery of the standard blues tempos and arrangements, and while his playing and writing were derivative, they were charged with the barely controlled emotion that characterizes great blues. All of Green's work displayed creditable restraint, unlike much British blues. Arrangements were dry and spare—Spencer, in fact, laid out completely on Green's featured tracks—but McVie (who'd come over soon after "Believe My Time Ain't Long") and Fleetwood were as solid and sympathetic a rhythm team as any trio needed. Green also played some suitably parched harmonica on "Looking for Somebody," which rather daringly had no guitar at all. "I was very purist in those days," Green recalls, "and the freedom of having our own band let me do things like (Howlin' Wolf's) 'No Place To Go' and 'Looking for Somebody.' That's how I wanted the band to sound."

P ETER GREEN'S FLEETWOOD MAC, AS THE first album was called, moved into *The New Musical Express'* top fifteen albums in February, 1968, and it remained there for twenty-three weeks. That kind of reception was incredible for a strict, "pure" blues recording, especially in the context of the times, when the Beatles had already crowned rock music with the elaborate *Sgt. Pepper's* and Jeff Beck was turning the blues upside down with *Truth*. But Green and company were quick to join in the fray between "commercialism" and "purism." The British press, with its tendency to classify and specify whenever possible, gave them a purist tag, and the album definitely *was* blues, but Green was also careful to leave his band's options open. He reviled the "sick people" who cared only about the type of guitar strings he would use for the next twelve-bar shuffle. As Mick Fleetwood says, "I think the musical rules of the blues only appealed to Pete as an avenue to other things he could express himself through." Mike Vernon points out that "Peter wasn't conscious of playing a solo and realizing it sounded like B.B. King or someone. He didn't even listen to records very much."

The second single was "Black Magic Woman," the tune that later made Santana a worldwide juke-box staple. Listening to Fleetwood Mac's definitive ver-

Peter Green and John McVie.

sion—it was written by Green—one realizes that Carlos Santana not only adopted the lyrical minor-key, quasi-blues arrangement; he also directly copped some of Green's sinuous guitar lines. Green himself, however, professed an admiration for the Santana treatment.

Jeremy Spencer was nowhere to be heard on "Black Magic Woman," and it was a tendency that would become more and more frequent: when he wasn't out front, he usually didn't play at all. Then as now, such developments weren't analyzed or even discussed—they were simply accepted as the natural course of things.

Mick Fleetwood: "He just sort of withdrew and became like he was on stage, another band within the band. He was happy, we were happy."

"Jeremy was basically very lazy. We had a hard time even getting him out for gigs, because he'd be watching TV or something, and a lot of the time he'd still be wearing his slippers and dressing gown when he got in the van. And he had these incredibly funky old guitars. He was obviously a rather small gentleman, and not very strong, and all the tuning pegs were so rusted, so fucked up, that I used to have to take a set of pliers and turn them for him until the guitar was in tune. And this was on stage! Give Jeremy half a chance, he wouldn't do anything. Very dreamy."

T HE SECOND ALBUM, *MR. WONDERFUL*, added little to the impression left by the first. The format was the same—a mixture of original and reworked blues—but the band was this time augmented by a horn section that included tenor saxist Johnny Almond, as well as pianist Christine Perfect (the future Mrs. John McVie) from Chicken Shack, another Blue Horizon unit. The additional musicians made for a murkier and more heavy-handed sound than that afforded by the very stark arrangements of the first album, but *Mr. Wonderful* did have a rather authentic ambience. According to Vernon, that was no accident.

"That was something we worked on within the band. Jeremy of course was very keen on re-creating the strict Elmore James sound, which was very hard to do, because we really didn't know what went into the original. But Mike Ross, the engineer, and I spent quite a lot of time maneuvering amps and microphones to try and get that authentic sound. The horns weren't perfectly in tune, which is synonymous with a lot of the Chicago blues records, and they weren't always in time, either. But these were all things, you know, that were very much part and parcel of the business of making blues records in America in the

Fleetwood Mac **Mr. Wonderful** *album cover, Nov. 1968.*

'40s and '50s and prior to that. It was the poor quality of some of those recordings that Jeremy wanted to emulate. It was kind of hard—there we were, trying to make high-fidelity recordings, and someone in the band was telling us to do the opposite. But I'll admit that we created an atmosphere that you might not have gotten with a high-fidelity recording."

Green, always the equitable one, evenly split the album's twelve cuts with Spencer. But the latter's sodden slide numbers were by now merely tedious, four of them starting with the same, standard Elmore James "wadda-da wadda-da" riff. Green himself solidified his credentials as a fiery but tasteful guitarist and singer. What's more, when he sang "You know, life can be so sad/Sometimes you just sit right down and cry," or "I can't stop my mind wanderin' back to those days when I was just a downtrodden kid" (from "Trying So Hard To Forget"), it was apparent that he was truly singing about himself. Peter Green from the east end of London seemed to regard his life as a struggle from the very beginning.

Mick Fleetwood: "I guess Peter really felt that way, and unfortunately for him, he probably said he did. He often got misquoted, but he asked for it. He used to put his head on the block every five minutes. He was desperately trying to get into a lot of things, but as soon as he'd gotten into something he'd be out of it at the other end. So he ended up going 'Oh, noooo' about a lot of things he probably *had* said. In the early days he wasn't particularly good at expressing himself. I remember saying to him, "The best thing, Pete, is to only say something when you know you've spent a long time researching it and you know you really feel that way. If you don't, people will end up not listening and making up their own stories."

27

A THIRD ALBUM'S WORTH OF MATERIAL RE-corded by the original quartet, not released at the time but now available in America as "*The Original Fleetwood Mac*," served to reaffirm Vernon's contention that "it would be very hard to find a purer band than Fleetwood was. They were pretty much in the format of B.B. King, the Chicago school or the Elmore James school, and you can't get much purer than that in terms of contemporary blues. They were the leaders of quite a large number of English blues bands." Fleetwood Mac's follow-up 45 to *Mr. Wonderful* was "Need Your Love So Bad," a slow blues by Little Willie John. Green hadn't heard the original, recalls Vernon, but he built an arrangement from B.B. King's version. Vernon had previously worked with Mickey "Guitar" Baker, an American, and he induced him to come over from Paris to arrange the accompanying string track. The result was a feeling not unlike that of King's "The Thrill is Gone," and the tune did adequately on the British charts. It was the last "pure" blues single the band would make, and as such it was only a hint of what Green would come up with next.

CHAPTER

2

RELEASED IN THE FALL OF 1968, "ALBAtross" was the fourth Fleetwood Mac single and it remains one of their consummate achievements. It was a guitar instrumental, in the finest tradition of "Apache" or especially Santo and Johnny's "Sleepwalk." With Fleetwood's mallets spraying waves of cymbal and McVie tending a throbbing pedal point, the rhythm section was the personification of the slow, graceful beating of the giant bird's wings. Green overdubbed layers of softly colored guitars bending plaintively in harmony, not a note in excess, not a phrase out of place. It was an inspired piece of music. As Mike Vernon says, "There was a certain magic about it that I don't think the band has captured since. Quite honestly, I don't think any band could."

After two albums of straight blues, "Albatross" took people by surprise—even Vernon, their producer,

31

was "a bit shocked." But Mick Fleetwood suggests that "it was no big trip—things like 'The Supernatural' were really early 'Albatross.' And those songs showed Pete's true colors, what he actually had to offer."

Whatever it was, it was popular, and when the band returned in January from a late 1968 U.S. tour, the song was number one in the U.K. Fleetwood recalls the effect success had on them: "We used to be 'just the lads in the band,' and so on. Then suddenly we had a hit record, which was pure accident—someone decided to use it for a documentary, and the next thing you know the BBC had made a film of it, lots of birds flying around, and it was a hit. We didn't know fuck all about it. We were the same band. It was just a song in our act."

After recording "Albatross," but before leaving for America, the group added a third guitarist, 18-year-old Danny Kirwan from Brixton. Green and Fleetwood heard Kirwan's trio, Boilerhouse, at London's Nag's Head. At their recommendation, Vernon booked Boilerhouse into his own blues club, which was uncoincidentally called the Blue Horizon; he soon recognized that Kirwan "had a guitar style that wasn't like anyone else I'd heard in England. It reminded me of Lowell Fulson—there was a certain vibrato in the fingerwork that was quite unusual. And he had a really nice, melodious voice."

Like the Levi Set Blues Group, Boilerhouse was weakened by its rhythm section. After persuading him to leave his old mates behind, Fleetwood and Green helped Kirwan audition new musicians, but nothing proved satisfying. In the end he joined

Albatross band 1968 (l. to r.) John McVie, Danny Kirwan, Mick Fleetwood, Jeremy Spencer, Peter Green.

Fleetwood Mac, which Mick says "was in the back of our minds anyway."

The first album with any Kirwan material on it came out, oddly enough, in America. Called *English Rose* and featuring an outrageous cover shot of Mick Fleetwood (as had the English *Mr. Wonderful*), it was a combination of cuts from *Mr. Wonderful*, "Albatross," "Black Magic Woman" and four tracks with the new guitarist. Of these, two were truly superior music: "Jigsaw Puzzle Blues" and "One Sunny Day." They were blues, but only generally—"Jigsaw," an instrumental, betrayed Kirwan's professed Django Reinhardt influence as it flowed smoothly from major to minor through three key modulations, while "One Sunny Day" was built around some crackling riffs that were as much rock as they were blues. Right from the outset it was apparent that he and Green were a wonderfully matched pair of guitarists who would assume the creative yoke of the band.

One product of the 70's has been bands who can mechanically reproduce every splendid note on their albums in live performance. Fleetwood Mac was always an exception. They thrived on their club and concert gigs as an outlet completely separate from records. The stage was their natural milieu, a place to get loose, to stretch out, to enjoy yourself without the pressures of being perfect for taped posterity.

This writer had the good fortune to take in a couple of concerts in Chicago on that same U.S. tour in late '68, and the charisma of this band was a revelation. The first set was their standard one—"Albatross" the centerpiece among lots of blues, Kirwan's and Green's guitars prodding and provoking each other in rave-ups like "Like It This Way"—and it was a good showcase for the unfamiliar American audiences. But the second set was something else entirely. They came out reeling drunk, and Jeremy Spencer ran through a series of utterly salacious Elvis routines complete with appropriate hip thrusts and greasy hair, sneering and strutting the stage like the King himself in miniature. He even had his own little gold lamé suit. By the time two or three in the morning rolled around, the few remaining stalwarts in the audience (in an inspired bit of booking, Fleetwood Mac was on a bill with Muddy Waters) had been treated to a febrile and fun display of blues and good ol' rock n' roll, drunken but forceful and featuring Jeremy Spencer as few in America ever heard him. Old rock and roll was Spencer's other great love, but the bulk of his hilarious parodies were restricted to the band's concert appearances. Only one "live" album—*Merely a Portmanteau*, it's called—has made it into Fleetwood Mac's recorded legacy, and it's a bootleg at that. But in the grooves of that record lie a hint of Spencer's appeal as a performer.

BEFORE RETURNING TO ENGLAND FROM that tour, the group took part in two recording projects. The first, known as *Fleetwood Mac in Chicago* or *Blues Jam at Chess* and organized by Vernon and blues magnate Marshall Chess, matched them with some great black bluesmen, including Otis Spann, Willie Dixon, Buddy Guy and Walter "Shakey" Horton. It was a rare opportunity for the Englishmen to play with musicians who had obviously influenced them so much, but John McVie remembers the sessions as being "a drag, because most of the black cats had the typical opinion of Whitey playing the blues. Look at my pictures on the cover and you'll know exactly how I felt." For his part, Peter Green recalls that "I didn't so much want to play with the bluesmen as to hear *them* play. But once we got going, I didn't care what they thought of me. I was just happy to be playing."

The Chess sessions were followed by another blues album, this one done in New York and featuring Otis Spann backed by McVie, Kirwan, Green and drummer S.P. Leary. These two records marked the band's final forays into pure blues.

Next came "Man of the World," second in the line of four singles that were not only Peter Green's but some of Fleetwood Mac's all-time best work. "Man of the World" was nearly a year in the making, Green recalls, and it confirmed what "Albatross" had already demonstrated: Green had a personal vision of his music that far transcended the blues idiom. He himself calls it "completely uninfluenced," while Vernon says that it "was a step in a particular direction, even though a radical departure from the blues format, and I suppose it led to what the band is now. Undeniably, they were getting more attention and more sales, so who was I to argue?"

"Man of the World" was a simple song, spotlighting some of Green's most world-weary singing and lyrics to match. Even so soon after the first flush of success, he was putting himself through some troubling disillusionment:

> Guess I've got everything I need,
> I wouldn't ask for more—
> And there's no one I'd rather be,
> but I just wish that I had never been born.

These were some strong sentiments for a burgeoning rock star, but Green meant them. In the background his guitar sang like a desolate pedal-steel, reinforcing the words with a yearning of its own.

Sometime after "Albatross," the group's management and Blue Horizon Records had what Mike Vernon will only say were "some legal hassles," resulting in "Man Of the World" being issued on the Immediate label. For the next album, *Then Play On*, Fleetwood Mac signed with Warner Bros./Reprise, their present company, and Green, for one, was skeptical about it: "I was the last to agree to leave Blue Horizon. I was quite happy there, and I didn't like leaving just for more money. I said to the rest of the guys, 'Watch out. There'll be a comeback from this.' " In any case, the break with Vernon and Blue Horizon meant the lessening of the heavy blues input, and with it went the predominance of "live in the studio," atmospheric recordings. The band began producing themselves, using the miracle of overdubbing extensively for the first time.

The blues was the first and last music Fleetwood Mac played that relied repeatedly on certain structural restrictions and stock changes. After "Albatross," things were wide open, and the group simply played whatever songs the various writers had that seemed suitable, whatever *felt* right, whether it was bluesy or not. They became, in Mick Fleetwood's words, "not just a blues band, but a musical band."

When it came to specific ideas about the content of *Then Play On*, Fleetwood says, "We knew we couldn't just make another album like the others. We didn't have an exact concept of what we were going to do, but we knew what we *weren't* going to do, and that was put out another record of Jeremy singing Elmore James." Green concurs, admitting that "Jeremy didn't have anything to contribute." Indeed. Spencer didn't have a single solo spot or songwriting credit on the entire album. A Spencer EP ("extended play" disc) was planned as a supplement to the twelve-inch release, but that was shelved in favor of his subsequent solo album. In the meantime, the rest of the group directed a well rounded and ambitious recording, rich in various musical textures and currents.

Mick Fleetwood: "We just went in and made the album—Pete knew pretty much what he wanted to do." Like Spencer before him, Danny Kirwan was given lots of space for his own songs: "Pete could

37

have done all the writing, really, but he gave Danny half the album to do, and Danny couldn't believe it. It was another example of Pete trying to steer people away from the big Peter Green image. No one even knew who Danny was."

Kirwan didn't quite make the most of his opportunity, but he did come up with a couple of fine tracks. "My Dream" was a stately instrumental with a flowing melody and intelligent interplay of a few succinct ideas. (In the course of his years with Fleetwood Mac, Kirwan wrote about five of the best rock instrumentals around, including this and "Jigsaw Puzzle Blues." They were partly the result of his difficulty with writing lyrics.) Another Kirwan song on *Then Play On*, a bluesy little guitar-vocal duet with Green called "Like Crying," was very different but no less effective.

Kirwan was skilled at suggesting a variety of guitar shadings by commingling acoustics and electrics, but songs like "When You Say" and "Although The Sun Is Shining" had fatuous lyrics and empty "la-la" melodies. Even so, his cotton-candy leanings were merely a sign of what were then immature writing habits. He later forged a remarkable style of his own that effortlessly matched the ballad feeling with the rock sensibility.

As for Green's *Then Play On* contributions, one of them was to lead Fleetwood Mac into some of the hardest rock music they've ever played. Best known was "Rattlesnake Shake," which was based on a blues progression but delivered as bone-crunching rock. The song was perhaps a little, ah, weighty, but Green proved he could play rock guitar with the bite of a mailman's nemesis.

Green had an instrumental of his own, "Underway," a floater that was nicely reminiscent of Jimi Hendrix's sound excursions. But of all the sides of himself that he revealed on the album, most striking was his rapidly growing *angst*.

"Before the Beginning" and "Closing My Eyes" (played by Green alone) came from the same depressed spirit that had spawned "Man of the World." The former two were almost painfully introspective, pinpointed by Green's anguished vocals and the sting of his guitar; "Before the Beginning" was one of his most powerful efforts. But the real key to his alienation—and whether that alienation was purely self-imposed or truly justified is a matter of speculation—was "Show Biz Blues." Perhaps the music itself, as he accompanied himself on electric slide guitar while a tambourine kept time, was a wishful throwback to the not-so-far-gone days before "Albatross" and The Big Time, when all he had to do was play the blues. The lyrics told their own story, in "Tell me anybody, now do you really give a damn for me?" or "You're sittin' there so green/But believe me man, I'm just the same as you."

Green had never been crazy about all the attention, continually understating his role in the band. But stardom in the U.K., even more so than in the U.S., meant that the fans hauled out their magnifying glasses to find out not only what brand of fuses went into a musician's amplifier but whether he sugared his cereal and liked women with shaved legs. Green had a magnetic personality, one that inspired a lot of that kind of treatment, but he was clearly uncomfortable with it.

Green now says that he "was going to leave the

group before 'Oh Well' [the third great Green single, released about the time of *Then Play On*], but Clifford Davis, our manager, persuaded me to stay on for the sake of the rest of the guys. You know, I wasn't out for success. I could take it or leave it—it wasn't anything that could hold me. I decided I would stay, but I wanted to move on to something new."

Despite the reservations of some critics, *Then Play On* did very well in Britain, reaching as high as number five on the charts in November, 1969; it was also the first Fleetwood album to sell more than 100,000 copies in America. It was a period that John McVie remembers as his most enjoyable time prior to their current success: "We had settled into a certain groove, when you get the feeling that your band is probably the greatest rock and roll band in the world. We had a confidence, a knowledge, a rapport with our audience."

Compounding the success of the album was the simultaneous ascension of "Oh Well." This one was Green's magnum opus—at nine minutes in length, its two parts took up both sides of a 45—and it was eventually considered important enough by Warner Bros. to include on new editions of *Then Play On*.

The first section of "Oh Well" was a very cleverly organized rock song. It had a signature riff played alternately and collectively on Green's classical and electric guitars and by the whole band, some of Green's best lyrics ("Can't help it 'bout the shape I'm in/I can't sing, I ain't pretty and my legs are thin/But don't ask me what I think of you/I might not give the answer that you want me to"), and a furious instrumental break characterized by the same sort of

Peter Green 1970.

dogfight guitar playing heard on the "Madge" jams from *Then Play On*.

After all that, Part 2 was the unexpected frosting. Green's classical guitar and cello work were framed in a long, artfully arranged and very romantic "movement." He was no classical virtuoso, but he had a good touch for simple themes reinforced by some lovely recorder playing (by Green's girlfriend at the time). Green recalls that he had been listening to a lot of Ralph Vaughn Williams' (20th century English composer) work, which helps account for the classical bent. And with part 1 added, "Oh Well" was a certified tour de force.

T HE RECORD THAT PROVED TO BE GREEN'S last with Fleetwood Mac came from an inspiration almost frightening in its impact. "I woke up one night," says Green, "sweating heavily and feeling like I couldn't move. I just felt terrible—and it wasn't that I was sick." That night he produced "The Green Manalishi," a song that Green says "was written out of fear, mostly. I think I realized at the time that it was very powerful stuff."

He was right. "Manalishi" was primeval in its force, driven by Fleetwood's relentless drumming and Green's power-chording and laced with eerie guitar solos. He had had a certain fascination with the otherworldly since "The Supernatural" in his Mayall days, and "Manalishi" was rife with images of darkness and arcane devilry. Green himself says it was about Satan, who "comes creepin' around, making me see things I don't wanna see." But it might not be too far-fetched to suggest in retrospect that the imagery was really cloaking his regard for his audience and basic position within his chosen field.

42

Before, it was "I Need Your Love So Bad"; now it was "Can't believe that you need my love so bad" and "All my tryin' is up, all your bringin' is down."

Peter Green quit Fleetwood Mac in the spring of 1970, in the wake of "The Green Manalishi's" success. What appeared at the time to be a totally unexpected move really wasn't so shocking. He had been restless for a while; the ambitiousness of "Oh Well," he says, was an indication of the boredom within the confines of a simple rock band that had made him want to leave before. Articles mentioned Green's increasing guilt over his role as a popstar, as well as his alleged desire to study the Bible. Clearly, a change was imminent.

The group's manager at the time, Clifford Davis, writes: "In May, 1970, Peter told me privately that he felt it was wrong that a group of entertainers such as Fleetwood Mac should earn such vast sums of money when, in fact, other people in the world didn't have enough to eat. He put to the band the following proposition—that all profits other than running costs earned by the band be given to needy people by way of donating to various trust funds, etc. Fleetwood and McVie did not wish to go along with this line of thought, and although Peter respected their decision, he felt he could not longer be associated with the band merely for his own financial ends. Peter Green... has given vast sums of his own private money derived from his songs to various charities such as Dr. Barnardo's Homes and Save the Children Fund."

Green's own explanations: "Yeah, I wanted to have a charity group, earning no money over the top, and give my money to starving children in Biafra and things like that. I also wanted at one point to go live in a commune in Germany. But that was after I'd taken some acid.

"I thought I had too much money to be happy and normal, and I got sort of panicky, I guess. Thousands of pounds is just too much for a working person to handle all of a sudden, and I felt I didn't deserve it. I didn't want any more."

John McVie recalls that he *did* at first go along with Green's charitable designs, because "there was no reason not to." He later revised his decision after realizing that the proposition "was coming from a space cadet, a guy who'd just been given lots of acid." But Mick Fleetwood's judgement was a bit harsher: "Pete was desperate to find a reason to carry on in the band. It was totally naive, and I didn't want to do it. I was earning a living, and we weren't making any fortunes, anyway. It was a pipe-dream, a sort of 'Why can't everyone be friends?' attitude. It was an overture to make himself valid."

Fleetwood's explanation for Green's overall disaffection is more earthy than Davis.': "He was always very preoccupied with being 'the downtrodden kid from the east end,' and I thought it was a load of crap. It was like a big chip on his shoulder. I wanted to tell him, 'Look, it has nothing to do with you. You are what you are, no matter what your background is. You're talented, and you're really lucky you can go out and do something.'

"Pete was very ambitious when he started, maybe overly so. He was so intent on making it, this 'I'll show you' thing, which I could never understand. When we

44

got successful, I thought it was great to be doing what we wanted to do—that's it. But for him it was a much bigger deal, like proving himself. When he'd finally gotten what he'd been fighting for, it's like it turned around and hung him. Towards the end he was reaching out to weird people outside the band who were sort of nurturing him. He was just not together."

Mick describes Green's quitting as "a very guilt-ridden decision, I think, like 'Now that I'm successful, I've got to do something with it.' He was a classic example of a very powerful person surrounded by yes-men, none of whom, me included, could tell him he was really only talking out of his bottom." But Green himself, while admitting that "I wanted to do something good and useful with my life, and I didn't think playing was it," also contends that "it had nothing to do with business or money or anything in particular. I just wanted to be free, with time to myself to jam with other people. It wasn't that I was tired of playing the hits—I never was—but I wanted to play with anyone and everyone.

"The whole thing was getting too serious, and I didn't want it. The thing is, my idea of success was just going on stage, or having a nice guitar, or jamming with someone at your house. I never cared about continuing the success. People who didn't come from a poor background, where you have to work your whole life, can't understand why you're not bowled over by success. It wasn't everything to me; it didn't mean I'd dedicate my life to having gold records. For me, the achievement wasn't having a popular record out—it was just having the music on tape in a good version."

After releasing one album (*The End of the Game*) and several singles, Green fell quickly out of the

English music scene. For a long period, and a strange period it was, he gave up music completely. The reasons for that are not clear, but it seems that he came to seriously question the advisability, spiritually speaking, of continuing to play. He worked for three months in a cemetery, doing what he calls "grave maintenance." In a move that Fleetwood calls "as near as he could get, being an untrained person, to helping suffering people," he also worked as a hospital orderly for a time, as well as holding down gigs pumping gas and in a wallpaper warehouse. He was a man without much direction.

Green now speaks candidly and without shame about several unsavory incidents in the years following his Fleetwood Mac stint. At one point, he says, he smashed some furniture in his parents' house, for no apparent reason, and spent three months in London's West Park Hospital for observation. "My mom was very frightened is why I went in," he says. "To this day I don't know why I did it. The vibes in the house just got horrible. It was something to do with eating too much food." (He had put on a good deal of weight after leaving the band.)

I N LATE 1976 (THE PREVIOUS INCIDENT WAS somewhat earlier), Green and Clifford Davis, still his manager, had a fight on the telephone in which Green "threatened to shoot him." Davis took it seriously, and when the police came to check out the situation, Green admitted that he did in fact own a gun ("I couldn't tell a lie. I had used it once for hunting."). The police took him to prison for some six weeks, where he underwent psychiatric testing while waiting to go to court. Typically, Green now describes prison as "a great life—plain, ordinary food and ordinary people. I'll tell you, being in there with rogues and drunks and thieves was a great experience for an old blueser like me."

His sentence put him in Horton Hospital for a few months, where he remembers getting frequent injections of drugs; "because of that I really started to get a bit melancholy." Later he went to another institution, The Priory, "where all the rich people go. I was dying of boredom. Made a hobbyhorse for my niece." Eventually he was released.

It was obviously a low point in the life of a musician whose creativity had once flourished, and his old mates, particularly Fleetwood, were perplexed and upset by his behavior. At about the time of the incidents related here, Fleetwood said with more sadness than anger that "Pete is completely aimless now. He was so motivated, so positive before. The few times we've seen him, he's been the complete opposite, a depressant on everyone around him."

In the past year, the situation has taken an encouraging swing for the better. As 1977 wore on, reports were that he had improved, and in December of that year he came to Los Angeles, where Fleetwood Mac has its offices. Mick spoke with relief about Green's easy-going, no pressure nature, mentioning that "Peter can even laugh about the jails, the hospitals and the rest of it." Green concurs: "I used to be a very active, very intense guy. Now I'm more into a relaxing trip."

Green was married to Jane Samuel at Mick Fleetwood's L.A. home on January 4, 1978 (Mick's wife, the former Jenny Boyd, was matron of honor, assisted by their two daughters), and he expressed his desire to "have children as soon as possible" and perhaps live in America. He was healthier and more positive than he'd been in some time. But perhaps most heartening was the news that he had once again taken up the guitar. "I just found myself falling back into it," he recalls. His trip to Los Angeles not only included a walk down the proverbial aisle; he and producer Peter Vernon-Kell also worked on setting up a domestic distribution deal for Green's new record. Fleetwood describes the material—which included a single, "Refugee," written in Peter's Fleetwood Mac days—as "not nearly as meandering as what he was doing a while ago. One instrumental sounded kind of 'Albatrossy.'" Green's return to recording and playing is long overdue.

In England, the departure of Peter Green was little short of a major national tragedy, and Fleetwood Mac didn't regain the popularity abroad that it enjoyed with him until six or seven years later. He dominated the British perception of the group. When subsequent line-ups, even the successful Buckingham-Nicks band, came to England, the press was more interested in Green's whereabouts than in the current Fleetwood Mac's activities. In part, it was the die-hard blues stigma, and people didn't forget that he had been primarily responsible for the string of superb hit singles. But perhaps the most cogent explanation of the Peter Green myth is offered by Christine McVie:

"The reason all this mystique and enigma hangs around Peter is that he did a very sensible thing: he dropped out just when people wanted more of him. He had just changed his musical direction, and I think he was frightened of all the power he'd attained. In England, Peter Green *was* Fleetwood Mac, but all of a sudden he was gone. It was like leaving everyone crying out for that last piece of lemon meringue pie."

Jane Samuel Green and Peter Green on their wedding day Jan. 4, 1978.

Kiln House album cover painted by Christine McVie.

Kiln House *band 1970, (front) Jeremy Spencer, John McVie (back) Danny Kirwan, Mick Fleetwood.*

CHAPTER 3

DESPITE GREEN'S QUITTING BEING regarded as nothing less than a Mick Jagger exile from the Rolling Stones, there was never a moment's hesitation about continuing Fleetwood Mac. There *was* some speculation that Danny Kirwan, considered Green's protege, might also leave, but he stayed on and they continued as a quartet.

Mick Fleetwood—always the most level-headed member—had assumed the spiritual and practical reins of the band, particularly behind the scenes. On stage, though, there was a definite void left by the absence of Green's tangible presence. Thus it fell to Kirwan and Spencer, neither of whom were, in Fleetwood's words, "front line sort of people," to fill the spotlight. And since Danny was especially retiring, it was mainly up to Spencer.

Fleetwood describes Spencer's transition from sometime clown to full-time front man: "Jeremy realized that in the cold light of day, he'd have to take up the slack left by Peter, who was a strong, powerful person. When Pete was in the band Jeremy leaned on him, and he hid his own personality behind some very convincing fronts. Pete's leaving made Jeremy wonder what the hell he was really doing. It probably helped put him on the old edge as well."

Most of Spencer's "convincing fronts," other than Elmore James, were revealed for the first time on vinyl in his solo album, a marvelous effort never issued in America. (In truth, the very first time had been a weird item on the flip side of "Man of the World." Known as "Somebody's Gonna Get Their Head Kicked in Tonite," it had Jeremy and the band masquerading as Earl Vince and the Valiants.) When *Jeremy Spencer* wasn't amusing, it was merely charming, and it made one remember what rock and roll should be all about: a good time.

To be really successful, any parody must have certain qualities, like a genuine respect and affection for its subject and, most important, accuracy; otherwise all sense of humor will be obscured. Spencer's LP had those qualities. It preserved the sense of tribute from the earlier Elmore James numbers, but went just far enough to be good parody.

In what amounted to a virtual rock and roll circus, *Jeremy Spencer's* tracks included send-ups of many musical heavies: Buddy Holly, Bo Diddley, the Beach Boys, Jan & Dean, and yes, even a few bluesmen. Of course, the record wouldn't have been complete without Jeremy's patented Elvis imitations. "The Shape I'm In" and "You Made a Hit" made faithful stabs at "Don't Be Cruel" or "All Shook Up"; but the real killer was "If I Could Swim the Mountain," a nod towards Presley's many lugubrious ballads, from gospel to "Love Me Tender." With a backing of acoustic guitar and pseudo-Jordanaires vocal, Spencer sang with a nearly unintelligible slur, murmuring the lyrics like a tranquilized bloodhound. It was a great ending to a great record.

If *Jeremy Spencer* had any glaring faults, one of them was certainly lack of an original vision. That wasn't a problem on what amounted to a novelty record, but it left some doubts as to his ability to make a serious contribution to Fleetwood Mac. *Kiln House*, the first post-Green group album, was a chance to determine if such doubts were well founded.

As it turned out, they were. But Spencer's "fronts" were so damned ingratiating that their lack of originality hardly detracted from what remains one of Fleetwood Mac's most attractive releases.

For his solo outing, Spencer had written most of his own material instead of simply adapting existing songs, and he used the same procedure for *Kiln House*. "This Is The Rock" was another Elvis take-off, and "Buddy's Song" again paid tribute to Buddy Holly (while giving composing credit to the latter's mother, a curiously generous gesture). "Blood On the Floor" was a satiric foray into another genre, country and western; its maudlin lyrics ("Well good-bye world, it's sad but true/Got a date with the hangman, I have to leave you") and cornpone vocal reaffirmed Spencer's imitative mastery.

Appealing though they were, his many masks gave no indication of what the real Jeremy had to offer. Only one tune on *Kiln House* came close to doing so, "a nice little song" called "One Together" and apparently written for his young wife. According to Mick Fleetwood, writing and singing about his own life was a nearly cathartic experience for Spencer, and he needed a good deal of encouragement to go through with it.

The genuinely creative moments on *Kiln House* belonged to Danny Kirwan, who came into his own on all accounts: writer, singer and guitarist. "Earl Gray" was another superb instrumental; here he was an aural craftsman, taking uncomplicated ideas and developing and ornamenting them into a cohesive whole. And just in case anyone thought he couldn't rock with the best, Kirwan came up with "Tell Me All the Things You Do," essentially a jam built around two or three precise vocal lines and guitar riffs. His searing solo work was more than enough to cloud the memory of Peter Green as Fleetwood Mac's guitar hero. But notwithstanding the excellence of "Tell Me" and "Earl Gray," Kirwan's principal *Kiln House* triumph was "Station Man." It rocked, but not hard; instead it was a subtly constructed series of dynamic movements, alternately burning and flowing, once again relying on the tasteful deployment of a few patterns and a simple vocal. Kirwan had few peers as an arranger.

CHRISTINE PERFECT HAD MARRIED JOHN McVie in 1968, and she was now brought in to supplement the vocals on *Kiln House* (she was also responsible for the terrific cover art). She formally joined the group soon afterwards—"I suppose it was a foregone conclusion after she married John," says Mike Vernon—and the foundation of Fleetwood Mac was solidified. Fleetwood and John McVie are these days the acknowledged nucleus, handling

Christine McVie with Chicken Shack.

Mac management, but Chris is equally vital to their endurance. "She's more mellow than Mick and me put together," says John. "She has a great ability to accept situations and put them in their proper order. That's her strength."

Chris was a rarity on the rock scene, a woman who not only sang but played. Like so many other English musicians, she'd been turned around by American blues and rock and roll; one of her first influences was Fats Domino, whose chunky chord style is echoed in her work even now.

As a pianist and occasional vocalist with Chicken Shack, one of Vernon's Blue Horizon bands, Christine usually left the limelight to guitarist Stan Webb. They were not much of an outfit. Webb was no Peter Green, and the torpid Chicken Shack records were unfortunately much more typical of British blues than early Fleetwood Mac had been. Nevertheless, it was with that band that McVie earned the respect of the likes of Peter Green as a player of taste and integrity.

Chicken Shack was not the place for McVie, and she

left for what proved to be an abortive solo career. In 1969 she enjoyed a popular single in England, a version of Etta James' "I'd Rather Go Blind," and was voted top female vocalist in *Melody Maker*'s annual poll. The album that followed, *Christine Perfect*, was a pleasant but bland amalgam of blues, R&B and a little pop (including Danny Kirwan's "When You Say") that met with good critical response but little sales activity.

McVie herself calls her solo career "a contrived farce. I didn't know much about my musical capabilities at that time, and I was being pushed around by a lot of people who thought they knew better.

"If it wasn't for Mike Vernon, I probably wouldn't even be in the business," Christine adds. "But he was trying to put me in too specialized a kind of trip, the black music kind of thing. I didn't even know I could sing or write very well. It wasn't until Fleetwood Mac that I first started putting songs together intelligently."

With Christine aboard, the *Kiln House* band did a couple of American tours. It was on the second of these trips, specifically in Los Angeles in February, 1971, that the second of the original Fleetwood Mac guitarists left the group.

The details of Jeremy Spencer's mysterious disappearance in L.A. are by now thoroughly documented. One afternoon he left the hotel on a shopping outing and simply didn't return, and after several frantic days he was finally located at an outpost of one of California's many religious sects, the Children of God. He had been accosted on the street, as many of us often are, and after what must have been one hell of a pep talk he became a convert. That was seven years ago, and remarkably, he is still a member of the Children.

On the surface, Jeremy's conversion was astonishing, a virtual 180 degree turnabout from the obstreperous and often obscene characterization of which Fleetwood Mac audiences and admirers had become so fond. But actually, like Green's quitting, it wasn't such a surprise, though more abrupt. He had been known to carry a Bible with him for some time, and at one stage it was reported that he and Green were working on a musical adaptation of the life of Jesus ("Another pipedream," says Fleetwood. "He should never have mentioned it in an article, because they knew it would never be done"). So the spirituality was there, however well it might have been disguised.

Spencer's susceptibility might also be explained in more general terms. His failure to express his real personality through his music may have been symptomatic of an inability to come to grips with himself. Religion provides many people with a solution to such problems, the theory being "find yourself through God," and perhaps Spencer found that kind of refuge with the Children.

He has not disavowed music since his defection. An album, *Jeremy Spencer and The Children*, appeared in 1972, and despite its predictably mindless lyrics, it was bright and enjoyable. These days he and his fellow worshipers have a band called Albatross, and yes, the circle *will* be unbroken.

The tour was completed with the surprising assistance of Peter Green, with whom they managed to bluff/jam their way through the remaining commitments. But clearly, another guitarist was needed. Judy Wong, a long-time friend of the group who now works for them, knew an American named Robert Welch, a player with a jazz-R&B background working in Europe, and he came over to England to meet the band.

WELCH'S UPBRINGING WAS A FAR CRY from those of the English members. He grew up in Beverly Hills, California, the movie star mecca; his mother was a radio actress in Chicago who later turned to TV (she even appeared in "Flipper!"), while his father went from radio and TV writing and producing to the movies, where he produced such immortal gems as "Pale Face" and "Son of Pale Face," both starring Bob Hope. Welch himself described his childhood as "a real Hollywood number, hanging around Paramount studios all the time, my parents throwing giant catered parties, the whole thing. It made me a little jaded and cynical before my time. I never had that real lust to make it—it was almost like coming in the back door." His songwriting was affected, as he freely admits: "I wrote things only from my own point of view, as if I was writing a poem and sending it to my twelve best friends. I figured everyone would know about these things."

Much of Welch's pre-Fleetwood experience came with the Seven Souls, a mostly black show band playing R&B and soul with a little pop mixed in, packing in the crowds at various L.A. venues. But instead of dreaming about becoming a rock star, he found himself wanting instead to go to Europe and live the Bohemian life, smoking plenty of opium and playing his own brand of sometimes inaccessible but sometimes outstanding rock/jazz/R&B/whatever.

Bob Welch.

Bob Welch (kneeling).

And that's exactly what he was doing when Judy Wong contacted him.

Christine McVie: "Before we met Bob, we tried a series of really embarrassing auditions with would-be Eric Claptons coming down to the house [the whole group lived together south of London]. But we just couldn't be so professional about it—y'know, 'What are your credentials' and all that. It was very difficult for us to say, 'Let's try a twelve-bar in D,' and listen to some guy wailing away. We'd say goodbye to these guys and realize we just couldn't do it.

"Bob never actually played a note. All we did was sit around and talk until dawn, and we just thought he was an incredible person. I remember saying to Mick that I didn't even care what his playing was like, he was such a good person. If we'd hated his guitar work it would have been a real drag."

Welch soon became aware of the band's unusual organizational methods: "I was expecting something like, 'Here, learn these songs and sing these parts,' but it was nothing like that at all. We just jammed for a long time, some blues once in a while. I thought they'd say, 'Look, this is what kind of band we are,' but I was expected to pull just as much weight as everyone. They didn't talk about direction, except to make it clear that they didn't want to do blues."

Assessing his stay in the band, Welch now says that "When I met them, they were going through sort of a weird phase, and it continued in that phase until after I left. I consider the whole period to be a floundering stage. They had begun as Green's band, a hot blues band, hit singles in Europe. Then when he left, Spencer and Kirwan didn't exactly know what

63

they were doing, and when I joined after Jeremy left, they really had no idea." Happily, that feeling of floundering was largely belied by the music.

After Welch joined in July of 1971, he says, "It turned out that the immediate plan was to go in and do a record. They said they didn't want to do any of Jeremy's things, so we worked on new material. We did do a couple of gigs first, in Holland, but it was mostly jam time, everyone getting drunk, totally uncontrolled like the early days."

FUTURE GAMES WAS THE FIRST ALBUM with both Welch's and Christine's active participation. Welch was represented by two songs, the title cut and "Lay It All Down." The latter was a shouter, reflecting his R&B experience and rather incongruous with the rest of the tracks, but "Future Games" was a treat. His playing was somewhat jazzier than other Fleetwood guitarists, but it also had the smoothly melodic qualities of Kirwan's and Green's work; and his nasal voice, while hardly outstanding, was an interesting contrast to the breathy tones of the English. Welch added a new dimension, but one that was certainly compatible.

Chris McVie had a couple of straightforward tunes (as opposed to Welch's and Kirwan's more complicated ideas) on *Future Games*. The rocking "Morning Rain" had some scorching Kirwan guitar and not much else of substance. "Show Me A Smile," on the other hand, was a lovely little ballad and the precursor of many more on later records. Her dusky voice lacked virtuoso range and technique, but she moved extremely well within its limitations.

Danny Kirwan's three *Future Games* contributions

The Future Games—Bare Trees band 1971. (l. to r.) Christine McVie, John McVie, Bob Welch, Danny Kirwan, Mick Fleetwood.

represented his musical acme. Bob Welch comments on Kirwan's fastidious recording habits: "Danny had a very specific idea of what he wanted to do in his songs—he was meticulous to the point of paranoia. It would take him days to get a solo right—he would have gone on for weeks perfecting one little thing if he'd been able to. He was always very isolated, very sensitive, and frankly he was very difficult to get to know."

All three of Kirwan's songs were aptly described by one English critic as "rock ballads." "Woman of 1000 Years" floated on a shining sea of languid, echo-laden acoustic and electric guitars, capped by his plaintive vocal and inimitable melodic sense.

"Sometimes" was a countryish song that focused on his effortless string-bending guitar style, and as Vernon had noticed long before, his finger tremelo was quite unique. The brilliant "Sands of Time" once again revealed how much use Kirwan could get out of a few well arranged ideas. Typically, he constantly shaped and reshaped the melodic lines, first singing them, then playing them (both alone and in harmony), then singing them again, the development always logical but never predictable. Each instrument played intuitively in support of the song's texture. Pure melody seemed to flow with incredible ease from every groove, woven together by the silvery threads of Kirwan's guitar.

Kiln House and *Future Games* were both reasonably successful in America, reaching the bottom of the top 100 and helping to put the group on a sales plateau consistently in the 250,000 unit range. *Bare Trees*, the album that followed, wasn't a lot more popular at the time, but it got receptive reviews and has become over the years one of the big favorites in the catalogue. The irony is that much of *Bare Trees* wasn't nearly as rewarding as its three predecessors. It appeared in the spring of '72, less than six months after *Games*, which might account in part for its higher complement of dispensable music.

Bob Welch and Chris McVie came up with a couple of their best-known songs, the former's "Sentimental Lady" and the latter's "Spare Me a Little of Your Love." In Welch's case it was also one of his best, a soft rocker with mellow Welch-McVie vocal counterpoint on probably the most commercial "hook" he ever wrote ("Sentimental, gentle wind, blowing through my life again/Sentimental Lady, gentle

Bare Trees Album (cover photo by John McVie).

one"). Welch didn't usually compose "catchy" material—like Kirwan, he tended to use a thematic, all-inclusive approach.

McVie was more a "pop" songwriter than the guitarists. Her love songs—many of them unqualified gems, some of them not a great deal different from others, all of them believable and none of them pure chaff—could be counted on as a refreshing demonstration of Fleetwood Mac's versatility. The country-tinged "Spare Me A Little," a good one but not one of her best, has for some reason become "a classic of mine. People go crazy, and I can't believe it. I had no idea it was so popular."

It was Kirwan who again dominated the proceedings, but the high expectations aroused by "Sands of Time" and "Woman of 1000 Years" weren't quite fulfilled. There was a shift from the melodic bounty of his previous work towards a more bluesy, riff-oriented style that wasn't nearly as distinctive. "Child of Mine" and "Bare Trees" reflected his signature arranging touch, and they were better-than-average rock songs by anyone's standards. But the limitations of the blues-scale melodies and squared rhythms of hard (and in the case of "Danny's Chant," heavy) rock seriously stifled his fertile imagination; "Tell Me All the Things You Do" and "One Sunny Day" had been the exceptions. A surfeit of busy guitar soloing, playing lots of notes in place of a few well considered ones, only compounded the banality.

Kirwan's better instincts got some breathing room in "Sunny Side of Heaven," the last of his great instrumentals and a credit to "World in Harmony," "Earl Gray" and all the others. Finally, there was ...ust," perhaps the most beautiful and fragile of the

Danny Kirwan late 1971.

"rock ballads," made all the more so by its use of the
opening stanzas of Rupert Brooke's poem:

> When the white flame in us is gone,
> And we that lost the world's delight
> Stiffen in darkness, left alone
> To crumble in our separate night;
> When your swift hair is quiet in death,
> And through the lips corruption thrust
> Has stilled the labor of my breath—
> When we are dust, when we are dust...

Kirwan had never seemed exactly happy, so it was
suitable that he choose such macabre words to put to
music (the poet himself was dead by age 28). He had
grown up without his father, perhaps resulting in an
increased dependence on his mother; and if he
harbored any resentment towards his father, it man-
ifested itself in a line from "Child of Mine": "I won't
leave you, no, not like my father did." Combine that
with the pressures of touring and being subjected to
extensive public scrutiny as an already sensitive
teenager, and one might find a clue to his reclusive
nature. To his credit, he made some fine music in spite
of it.

His frame of mind deteriorated on the post-*Bare Trees* tour. He became even more introverted and drank too excessively to remain a consistent live performer.

Bob Welch: "Sometimes he would be great, y'know, spot on, and other times he'd be completely out of it, cringing back at his amp, wasted out of his mind. I remember seeing him when he wouldn't eat for a week, just drink beer."

"By the end of the tour he'd just gotten too strange—it got to the point where there were too many weird scenes. There was one gig where he wouldn't even come out on stage. He was really pissed in the dressing room, and when we said 'C'mon, time to go on,' he flew into a rage, throwing his guitar, screaming and yelling. He went out to the mike mixer, watched the set and came up later and said 'It was a pretty good gig, a little out of tune here and there,' that kind of thing. It was really weird."

Mick Fleetwood: "I was the last mainstay, hoping he would pull out of it. But he just couldn't relax around people, and it made us feel very ill at ease. It became intolerable, everyone was so fucking tense. I finally admitted *I* couldn't take it either, and I had to be the one to tell him, to put him out of his misery. I knew he wouldn't understand, and he didn't—he asked why. It was horrible."

Manager Clifford Davis contends that it was only Fleetwood and Welch who "could not get on" with Kirwan. Chris McVie was once quoted to the effect that *she* and Kirwan had clashed. In any case, something had to be done; the tour was cut short and he was, says Davis, "politely fired."

Kirwan has released two solo albums in America in the five or six years he's been gone from the group. The first was the hopefully titled but disappointing *Second Chapter*. One track, "Ram Jam City," was an unusual (for him) "Scottish bluegrass" number with a rousing instrumental tag, while several others brought back that wistful voice and lilting guitar, but by and large, *Second Chapter* was pretty forgettable. It was obvious that Kirwan very much missed the backbone of support supplied by John McVie and Mick Fleetwood. Without them, the music had little more gravity than a helium balloon.

The second Kirwan album, known as *Midnight in San Juan* abroad and called simply *Danny Kirwan* when released here in '77, was more of the same: some attractive melodies, but delivered from so wimpy a stance as to barely command one's attention. By the time of this album's release, Clifford Davis had long since made Fleetwood Mac's abbreviated enemies list, yet he remained Kirwan's manager, and produced *Danny Kirwan*. In fact, the backup musicians were the very same crowd that played a role in the infamous "bogus band" scam, about which more in the next chapter.

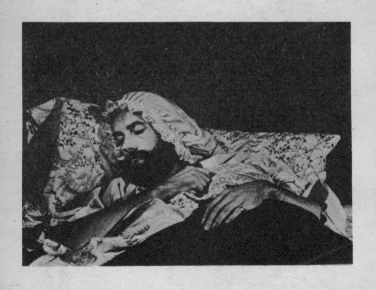

83

84

CHAPTER 4

THREE GUITARISTS HAD FALLEN BY THE wayside so far, all of them talented and at least one (Green) "important" enough that this departure would have been sufficient reason for *everyone* to pack it in. But still they endured, and with the dismissal of Danny Kirwan began the strangest period in Fleetwood Mac's quilted history. In the next two years they would record three albums, shrink from a sextet to a quartet and begin a marathon legal struggle that has yet to be fully resolved. Through all of it the name of Fleetwood Mac would sustain, while they unknowingly edged their way toward the kind of popular rewards that very few bands ever enjoy.

The initial reaction to Kirwan's demise was a collective sigh of relief, followed by some speculation as to his replacement(s). As Bob Welch recalls it, Clifford Davis had some ideas about who that should be: "There was a lot of pressure from Davis to be a 'star-quality,' headlining act. He saw bands like Deep Purple, Uriah Heep—macho, heavy bands with a lead singer strutting around the stage—and he thought we should have a front man." Davis himself refutes Welch's inferences, saying that "Mick Fleetwood was the instigator of Dave Walker joining the band, largely due to the departure of Peter Green, there being no forceful leader, and it was decided that Walker would fit that position nicely."

They had been accompanied on the *Bare Trees* tour by Savoy Brown. In Walker, who was Savoy's lead singer, they found someone who was likeable and who fit the front-man bill, and he was persuaded to join. Bob Weston, who had also been on the tour as a member of Long John Baldry's group, signed on as well. This aggregation went on another tour in late 1972, and then went back to England to record *Penguin*.

Bob Welch's comments about this latest Mac incarnation are partly a reiteration of his earlier feelings: "I guess the music had a certain aura to it, but we didn't feel it—we didn't feel the positiveness. Maybe you only feel it after the fact. But somehow, things seemed paranoid. It was the same after Walker and Weston joined."

Even though it "seemed like a good idea at the time," says John McVie, almost everyone now concurs that the hiring of Dave Walker was a mistake. Chris McVie's explanation: "Dave was great in Savoy Brown. But you try and get a guy like Dave Walker singing anything other than Howlin' Wolf or Freddy King or rock and roll boogie and he just didn't cut it. He wasn't terribly versatile, that's all, and he wasn't right for us."

That's putting it mildly. Walker's two numbers on *Penguin*—the album was named for John's favorite creature, some image of which appears on most records after *Then Play On* and is now used to represent their song publishing—were as egregious as a wart on Cybill Shepherd. The ersatz-Motown version of Junior Walker's "(I'm a) Roadrunner" was one of the worst tracks Fleetwood Mac has ever done. Walker shouted his way relentlessly through it, while the cymbal-less drums sounded as if they had been recorded off a transistor radio. Walker's own "The Derelict" was little improvement.

With Kirwan gone, Welch and Chris McVie dominated the original output. Though she calls *Penguin* "a really weird, out in the ozone kind of album," McVie contributed three fine songs. "Remember Me" was the first choice for a single, and while it never clicked as a hit, it had all the components: memorable melody, hook-filled chorus, concise arrangement. The rollicking "Dissatisfied" was even better, with Bob Weston adding a delightful slip 'n slide country guitar solo, while "Did You Ever Love Me" and its calypsoid steel drums felt just as good. It's a bit hard to understand why these songs garnered little or no attention on the AM radio circuit, especially in view of their stylistic similarity to recent hits like "Over My Head" and "Don't Stop." Any one of them would have been a breath of fresh air.

Welch, who also describes *Penguin* as "obscure," held up his end in equally admirable fashion. He had developed his own style by building a thickening musical environment on a couple of steady chord patterns that would complement his cerebral subject matter. Like Kirwan, he was a technician who "knew exactly what he wanted" in the studio; like Green, he had a fascination with the mystical ("I had an affinity for the old Peter Green stuff—maybe that's one of the reasons the band liked me"), though Welch tended to express it in more esoteric terms. His lyrics, with titles like "Bright Fire" and "Night Watch," could be a little self-conscious ("All through the dust and the green magnesium fire," or "He controlled the brimstone and the eternal fire"), yet they could also be nicely evocative ("He walled up the door to summer and cut the heart out of the spring"). His three tracks on *Penguin* worked as elemental mood music: fire and air imagery, watery guitar sounds.

One of Fleetwood Mac's strong suits has always been diversified material, and Welch's not very commercial songs provided a viable alternative to McVie's. "Revelation" was the most well conceived and well executed; it featured a bass solo, a real rarity for this band and played, no less, by Welch. "Revelation" and "Night Watch" also stood out from a percussive standpoint, the former with Fleetwood's agile congas and the latter with his African talking drum. What's more, "Night Watch" included a guitar track played by none other than Peter Green. Though he was uncredited, the Green sound was unmistakably there.

A FTER "ROADRUNNER" IT SEEMS HARD to believe that Walker's incompatibility wasn't realized right away. The *Penguin* lineup went on the road to support an album that looked to be a commercial stiff, then returned to England to record yet another one in the summer of 1973. It wasn't until *Mystery To Me* was partially completed, with some of its songs written for Walker, that they had serious reservations about him. According to Bob Welch (and the pattern of the band's existence),

Mystery To Me *band 1973 (l. to r.) Christine McVie, Mick Fleetwood, Bob Weston, Bob Welch, John McVie (front).*

the Walker situation was typical of Fleetwood Mac's laissez-faire approach. They have rarely pressured themselves into career decisions, a condition that has no doubt played a role in their longevity.

"We'd work everything out," Welch says, "but sometimes working it out took so long that by the time we got there it was too late. It took us months to decide things."

During the *Mystery* sessions, "Dave would go down to the pub and get drunk while we did the rest of the album, trying desperately to figure out what we could give him to do. The light finally dawned on us that we were throwing away what Fleetwood Mac had been, that we weren't Savoy Brown. It was an experiment that failed," and an amicable parting was arranged.

"John McVie wasn't nearly as involved in everything then as he is now," continues Welch. "He'd go to the pub with Dave and come back three days later. He was very paranoid about his playing—during *Mystery* he wanted to go to France and come back later to put on his bass parts, and we kept having to convince him to stay. He and Chris used to have a lot of ups and downs, I mean a *lot*. Then it was probably more downs than ups."

WELCH AND CHRISTINE "REALLY burned" rewriting material that had been intended for Walker, and the record was released in October. Out of the latest turmoil came another ambitious and varied (though uneven) work; like *Bare Trees*, its greater proportion of short, commercially aimed songs appears an unconscious reaction to the thematic bent of much of its immediate predecessor.

Christine could by now be expected to provide solid, often superb songs every time out, and this was no exception. "Believe Me" and "Just Crazy Love" were two more satisfying rockers, lively and tight around the edges, while "Why" was her showcase, the prettiest ballad she had written to that point. After a tasty Weston slide guitar intro (shades of Peter Green on "Show Biz Blues") it grew into a full-blown pop production number, complete with swelling strings, before subsiding into a gentle guitar coda.

Bob Welch really took charge of *Mystery To Me*, on the basis of six individual song credits and one collaboration with Weston/McVie. His eclecticism was given free rein, and while he wasn't always successful, he couldn't be faulted for exploring the limits of his imagination.

A couple of Welch's tunes were expendable, including the bogus reggae "Forever" (the collaboration) and the raucous future blues "The City"—the latter and "Somebody" indicated that Fleetwood Mac couldn't play funk much better than they had played soul. But three other tracks were more than ample compensation.

"Miles Away" cooked with as much punch as the earlier "Revelation," given life by McVie's propulsive bass (as Welch says, "He plays lines that you can listen to as a part, not just 'a bass line' "). "Keep On Going," with its sweeping minor melody, another surprisingly effective string chart and a great vocal by Christine, was one of Welch's very best *song* songs, one that could stand up by itself were it to have no elaborate accompanying arrangement.

The final, brightest jewel (and probably the most

brilliant *music*, period, that Welch has ever made) was "Hypnotized." Mick Fleetwood played a metronomic pulse under the cyclical chord pattern, while Chris McVie added swaying fields of electric piano and Welch colored in the edges with jazzy guitar octaves. The song's ambience so embodied its title that it nearly had an aura to it, soothing the listener into a groove that one wanted to last forever. Topped with its enigmatic lyrics about "a strange, strange pond" in North Carolina with "sides like glass, in the thick of a forest without a road" and "a place down in Mexico where man can fly over mountains and hills," "Hypnotized" was the pinnacle of Welch's explorations into "environmental" music, wherein the separate elements conspired in one transcendent whole.

Welch didn't mind taking verbal risks in his composing. He wrote his quota of love songs, but even they weren't ordinary ("Emerald Eyes is a mystery, she's my place of serenity").

Along with his recurring preoccupation with (super)natural phenomena, he could interpolate more topical ideas in his lyrics: "Don Juan goes up in a cloud of smoke/and all those Hare Krishnas turned out to be a joke" and "There's too much Warhol hangin' off the wall" came from "Miles Away." Welch had the most far-reaching intellectual curiosity of any Fleetwood writer before or since.

The *Mystery* group was one of the strongest in Fleetwood Mac's experience. The two guitarists worked well together, playing to each other's advantages. The songwriting was balanced, the music tight—it was a real *band*. They set out on another tour, not foreseeing that this line-up, too, would be shortlived.

92

Midway through the road trip it developed that Bob Weston was lasciviously allied with Jenny Fleetwood, Mick's wife. Since Mick knew he was being cuckolded, it soon became impossible for them to perform on stage together, so Weston was fired and the rest of the tour was cancelled. The remaining four members decided on an indefinite hiatus, Bob Welch says, "so things could settle down." Welch returned to L.A., and Fleetwood ("He was a basket case, not just because of Weston but because of overwork") went to Africa. They informed manager Davis that they intended to re-group in a few months (it was then late '73). Then "the shit really started to hit the fan."

CLIFFORD DAVIS, APPARENTLY UN-happy about yet another turnover, decided the situation could not wait several months; Davis himself does not comment extensively, but he refers to an article from *Let It Rock* magazine which indicates that "McVie had already stated he was going to leave the band at the end of the tour and Bob Welch was soon to be off with Lee Michaels," both of which allegations are denied by Fleetwood Mac. The article suggests that Davis was concerned that "the band could face a lot of lawsuits unless something was worked out quickly" regarding the canceled dates. Claiming ownership of the name "Fleetwood Mac" (or, as *Let It Rock* says, "acting only for their company, Fleetwood Mac Co., and not to save his own head"), Davis put together "The New Fleetwood Mac," comprised of members of various other groups in his stable, and sent them to America to complete the tour. No members of the real Fleetwood Mac were in any way connected with this new band; *Let It Rock's* statement that "Mick and Christine came to Davis and agreed to front a band put together around them" is categorically denied.

"The New Fleetwood Mac" tour was disastrous, as promoters and audiences alike were understandably irked at the masquerade. The real group had gotten wind of it, and "we finally succeeded in getting the bogus band off the road with a temporary injunction," Welch recalls.

Whether what Davis did was ethical or not is a serious bone of contention. Mickey Shapiro, a California lawyer now representing Fleetwood Mac, suggests some reasons why it may not have been:

"What you really have is not an altruistic move to save face and retain the group's good name by putting together this new band as an element of good will; you have a man profiteering off of an asset, which in this case is made up of a name. 'Fleetwood Mac' implies the participation of Fleetwood and McVie, and they weren't at all involved with it.

"Clifford Davis formed a company, and he may have had a piece of paper saying something about owning the name, but what about the public? When you talk about 'Fleetwood Mac,' you talk about an image in the mind of the public of what they're buying. You can't just freely trade that off, because when a guy puts down a dollar for A, he doesn't expect B."

The bogus band situation touched off a series of Dickensian suits and countersuits whose resolutions have now been pending for almost four years. According to Bob Welch, it highlighted "a feeling that we weren't getting all we should" from various royalties for which Davis, as manager, was responsible; as Shapiro puts it, "It was the event that turned the lights on for everyone to say 'Hey! Where have all these funds gone?' It disturbed the element of trust" that

had tacitly (and contractually) existed between Clifford Davis and Fleetwood Mac for some years.

Davis' side is that he is entitled not only to the management commissions which were part of his contract, but to recording and publishing royalties as well. Evidently he had personal contracts with band members (separate from the management contract) through which he published their songs, but they are being disputed under a doctrine which, says Mickey Shapiro, makes certain publishing agreements not legally enforceable. Fleetwood Mac also claims that the managerial agreement is now void due to a number of violations. Concerning recording royalties, Shapiro contends, "he has never, ever had any document whatsoever that gives him the right to negotiate recording rights on behalf of Fleetwood Mac." There are at this point hundreds of thousands of dollars in funds being impounded by Warner Bros.—how they will be distributed is contingent on the outcome of the case. Clifford Davis is no longer associated with Fleetwood Mac, and will say only that "a great injustice has been done to me."

The aftermath of the ersatz group's tour was that the real band's credibility became suspect. Promoters who had been burned were suspicious, and Warner Bros.; although "their sympathy was with the band," was extremely diffident when it came to renegotiating a contract—they did so directly with the band, and only when indemnified in the event of Davis' winning the case. For the band itself, Welch says, "it was a depressing situation—positive in that we had survived, but very paranoid."

WORK BEGAN ON A NEW ALBUM, aptly titled *Heroes Are Hard To Find*, in June 1974. No replacement for Weston was sought, and *Heroes* was made as a quartet. It was not a bad record by any means—there were some satisfying moments—but one could hardly blame them if their hearts weren't completely in it.

The main problem with *Heroes* was its facelessness—it sounded like too much other pop music. Chris McVie's title song and "Come A Little Bit Closer," the first marred by a lightweight horn track and the second an attempt to recapture the "Why" production-number quality, were just not performed with the conviction of her earlier work. Much more forceful were "Bad Loser" and "Prove Your Love," two more products of her simple and affecting dealings with the "me"and "you" of personal relationships.

Bob Welch, having already proved himself a more capable thematic craftsman than pop stylist, and no doubt recognizing his achievement with "Hypnotized," again worked at attaining the symbiosis of obscure lyrical notions and atmospheric musical settings that had made it so good. But where "Hypnotized" had been subtle and suggestive, "Bermuda Triangle" was pretentious in its lyrics ("You're feeling safe in your harbor/And everything seems certain/Right next to Palm Beach and Key Biscayne/Behind a velvet curtain") and uninspired in its music. "Coming Home," however, was built around an intriguing musical design and more fine octave guitar, and was again much closer to what one knew Welch could do.

The suspicion that Welch's enthusiasm was pretty much spent by the time *Heroes Are Hard To Find* had run its course proved justified when he left Fleetwood Mac in Dec. '74. Welch was tired and frustrated. He had worked hard to keep things afloat during the Clifford Davis scam, and after *Heroes*, "I was looking for a bigger indication that all the crap had been worth it. But as it was, we just turned over another page.

"I had come to the point whre I didn't feel I had anything else to offer the band; I had just burned it out. Faced with the prospect of making another Fleetwood record, I wouldn't have known what to do. "I had come to the point where I didn't feel I had anything else to offer the band; I had just burned it chugging along on one cylinder, and my attitude was that after four years of ups and downs, something had to give."

Welch had been an integral part of Fleetwood Mac, more so, say Mick Fleetwood and Christine McVie, than Peter Green. Describing Welch's development in his years with the band, Fleetwood comments, "Bob always used to wish that he'd had the same type of background as us in a lot of ways, because it leads you more to an emotional content rather than a technical one, and that to me is the most important thing—in anything, really, when you get down to it. He'd be practicing for hours, doing all these jazz licks, then suddenly it didn't really mean anything. I think while Bob was in the band, he got to understand that side of it and appreciate a sort of angle that he never got involved in before, which is just a simple, honest approach to music. It's a way of having sympathy for other players, for not over-extending yourself; it's taste, really."

After leaving, Welch was involved for a couple of years with the trio Paris, along with bassist Glen Cornick. (Again, many things with Fleetwood Mac come full circle: Cornick was married to Judy Wong when she introduced Welch to the Mac.) Welch calls

Heroes Are Hard To Find band 1974 (l. to r.) Bob Welch, Mick
Fleetwood (in back), John McVie, Christine McVie.

the Paris venture "a cross between what I wanted to
do"—moody, jazz-tinged material drawn from the well
that inspired "Hypnotized"—"and what I thought
would sell." But it didn't, because the attempts at
commercialism were too often mired in pretension.
One senses that he was not entirely satisfied with
either of the two Paris albums, nor was he committed,
at least in spirit, to the band's future.

Welch's philosophy, like that of Fleetwood Mac itself,
has often been a passive one in terms of charting his
own future. While he was still with Paris, he once
commented that "it seems the less you make plans,
the more things will take shape. I'd like things to be so
you plan them out, but it usually doesn't work that
way. Things seem to be more vital when plans aren't
made." With Paris, vitality was one element that was
definitely missing, and Welch seemed to recognize

that. "I'm at a point right now where I don't really know what is satisfying," he said in late 1976, not long before Paris went the way of all flesh. "Every time you do something, it demands you do something else."

He did do something else, and the summer of 1977 saw him return to the Fleetwood Mac fold, insofar as Mick Fleetwood took over his managerial reins. A solo album called "French Kiss" appeared, on which Fleetwood, Chris McVie and Lindsey Buckingham, Welch's successor, contributed to a fine remake of "Sentimental Lady." McVie and Buckingham produced, while Buckingham handled the arranging, and the latter's crystalline twelve-string guitars and Fleetwood's powerful drumming helped make "Lady" a sizeable single hit for Welch.

Welch clearly lacked direction when he first left Fleetwood Mac, but his renewed association with Mick Fleetwood should help dissuade him from taking the line-of-least-resistance approach he seemed partial to with Paris. The change was already apparent soon after "French Kiss" was released: Welch, and often Mick as well, made the tedious rounds of countless radio stations, supporting the album with the enthusiasm and businesslike approach a serious career these days demands. And it's a good thing, too, because someone of his talents and intelligence deserves not to be inconsequential.

Fleetwood Mac 1975.

CHAPTER 5

MAYBE IT WAS INEVITABLE THAT AT SOME point in the band's evolution, Fleetwood and the McVies would be the sole survivors. These three, more than any of the guitarists, had come to embody Fleetwood's ethic of "a simple, honest approach to music."

Mick Fleetwood's family had always supported his musical aspirations. They were fairly prestigious in England: his father was a former wing commander of the Royal Army, while one of his sisters remains a member of the Royal Shakespeare Company.

Mick had unpretentiously molded his background into the leadership of Fleetwood Mac. As the group's manager, he was astute, practical, a diplomat. Most of all, he was refreshingly devoid of attendant bullshit as he surprised steadfast recording industry types who swore that he'd never be able to manage a

Mick Fleetwood.

John McVie.

big-time operation like Fleetwood Mac and still be able to play music. Now, as one watches him sit back at his drums, mouth wide open in concentration as he provides the kind of solidity that could anchor a dinghy in a hurricane, one knows that he has taken care of both business and music very well, thank you.

Mick's own assessment of what he brings to Fleetwood Mac's management is typically insightful, as he revealed recently in an interview with *Record World* magazine: "I feel responsible for the basic cord of what the band clings to, or does, and I feel safe in saying I'm responsible for initiating a lot of things. Most people thought it was going to be impossible. They just said, 'You can't do it, forget it. The only way your band is going to make it is to change the name.'"

Fleetwood didn't adopt the hustling, often obsequious but also imperious attitudes of many managers; as he himself said, "It's pure instinct, utter instinct. Every move that's ever been made was one where I said, 'Don't worry, it will happen,' and, touch wood, it has happened. It's like a little magic guiding star, and it has certainly turned out well. I'm not saying it's all luck; it's not. But I'm not a manager manager." Still, his straightforward attitude doesn't preclude a familiarity with the basic business of selling records: "Within reason, there's no point worrying about the album slipping off the charts; then you say, 'All right, it's happening, so what can we do about it,' and then you go out and tour, or you try to get more promotion to build airplay. That's not a big deal."

CHRISTINE McVIE HAD A MORE OBVIOUS musical upbringing, in that her father was a musician with a teaching degree and her grandfather had played the organ in Westminster

Christine McVie.

Abbey. She herself had gone to a special art school, then art college, and eventually earned qualification as a teacher, specializing in sculpture. She was window dressing at a London department store when the call came to join Chicken Shack (known at that time as Sounds of Blue), via Mike Vernon.

Christine was the one with the low profile. As she told *Record World*, "If I have any image at all, it's no image. Others have called me sort of a maternal type—it's not that I want to be a matriarch, but I'm certainly no sex queen, either. My role is campadre musician. I'm one of the guys, really." She was self-assured, but with no need to exploit the potential glamor that came with the pop music scene.

As a musician herself, not only a singer, Christine's role in Fleetwood Mac was unlike that of most women in bands, since she could jam as "one of the guys" and not have to leave the stage or fidget uncomfortably while the guitar players wailed away. Mainly, she still loved to play, sing and write after all her years on the road, and she was relaxed enough to deal with the rigors and tendency to self-destruct inherent in the rock and roll style.

JOHN McVIE WAS FLEETWOOD MAC'S FREE spirit, a traveler with a wry sense of humor and an affinity for fishing, scuba diving and various ecological concerns, such as the Jacques Cousteau Society; yet he has avoided involvement in certain other organizations, for as he says, "They spend too much time slaggin' each other off and criticizing Cousteau to ever get much accomplished." As a manual perfectionist, McVie's musical skills were right in line with other talents such as gourmet cooking, leather work and photography. He now has a house on Maui, Hawaii (at one point, he lived on a boat near L.A.), where he goes during breaks in touring and recording with the woman he plans to marry after his and Christine's amicable divorce is finalized.

McVie was perhaps the hardest to get to know, due to a cantankerous quality that sometimes accompanied his drinking, but he was a man whose trust one instinctively wanted to earn. He came to maintain a role secondary to Mick's in the management of Fleetwood Mac, but that was the way he wanted it. As he told *Record World*, "Mick enjoys doing it, and he's gradually come to the front. I don't particularly enjoy making phone calls and talking to accountants and all that. But Mick bounces off me—I give him my opinion and he weighs it with his, in terms of direction, or artistic layout of an album cover, how a tour should go, that sort of thing."

After a short period as a trumpeter when he was a boy, McVie took up guitar, which eventually gave way to bass. His first band—coyly named the Krewsaders, he recalls—played instrumental music fashioned after the Ventures and the Shadows, both of whom were immensely popular in England. After joining the Bluesbreakers in 1963, McVie stayed with John Mayall for more than four years, and now refers to him as "my mentor." And though it didn't seem obvious, McVie became a vital part of Fleetwood Mac's spirit. Softspoken, insightful and, like Mick, never taking it all too seriously, he embodies the band's perserverance.

A S IT HAPPENED, FLEETWOOD MAC WAS only a trio for about a week. Once again, acting as usual by instinct, they added new

121

members and continued. But this time it would be different. They didn't know it; how *could* they have known that the eighth time's the charm?

The comings and goings of Mac personnel had been fairly strange; after all, Peter Green as a hospital orderly and Jeremy Spencer on the road to Damascus are not the usual ex-rock star routines. Now there was the improbable joining of Lindsey Buckingham and Stevie Nicks. While perhaps not of the mythical proportions of Lana Turner at Schwab's Drugstore, it was still a classic Hollywood scenario: Struggling virtual unknowns found by established band, the two join forces and together they comet to the top.

Not long before Bob Welch decided to quit, Mick Fleetwood was checking around southern California for a suitable studio in which to record the *Heroes* follow-up. At Sound City in Van Nuys, engineer Keith Olsen happened to play him a tune called "Frozen Love," by Buckingham Nicks. It wasn't an attempt to sell Fleetwood on the music itself; it was simply meant as an example of Olsen's work and Sound City's capabilities (Stevie Nicks: "*Nobody*, unless he was totally crazy, would try and sell someone not only on a guitar player but a girl singer, too. Maybe one of us, but not the twin set!"). Nevertheless, Mick was as impressed by the duo as he was by the studio, and when Welch took out his walking papers Buckingham and Nicks were immediately contacted. The circumstances were a little unusual for this band. Whereas Welch had sat around for weeks before picking a note, Stevie and Lindsey were rehearsing and taking an active part in the music right away, even before they'd conquered their original hesitations about joining at all.

Lindsey Buckingham.

Stevie Nicks: "Mick called us right after Bob Welch left. He never said 'Do you want to audition' or 'Do you want to come over and we'll get to know each other' or anything. Right from the beginning it was 'Do you want to join?' We got together a couple of days later for a Mexican dinner, and it was 'Rehearsals start next week' and all that. All of a sudden we were rehearsing, and we went into the studio two weeks later."

A night and day turnabout for Buckingham and Nicks? Not entirely. It wasn't as if they were utter neophytes in the rock and roll world. Actually, they had paid some fairly hard-earned dues of their own.

B UCKINGHAM AND NICKS, LIKE WELCH BE-fore them, were Americans joining what was essentially an English band. Lindsey had grown up in Atherton, California. His brothers were swimming stars (Greg was a silver medalist at the 1968 Olympics in Mexico City), and Lindsey himself might be Mark Spitzing it even now were it not for the lure of music.

Buckingham was exposed to the classic rockers of the '50s at an early age, through his older brothers, and that music was a major influence. Having played guitar since age 7, he mastered finger-picking styles while retaining his love for good ol' rock n' roll. But despite his abilities, he never thought of himself as a future rock star: "For a long time I never really saw myself playing music for anything other than enjoyment. Even all through high school, I would go watch bands, and even though I probably played guitar better than people who were up there, I was just doing it for fun. I didn't really think about it in terms of trying to make it as a musician." It wasn't

124

until college that he made a serious commitment to music, and, in fact, he recalls having to make a decision between busting his ass for the water polo team or playing music.

These days, Buckingham has no trouble accepting the stardom that has rather rapidly come to him. Like all of Fleetwood Mac, he's utterly down-to-earth, unsurprised at the band's success without being at all self-conscious or arrogant about it. His devotion to the music is his driving force, and he perhaps works harder at it than any of the others.

STEPHANIE "STEVIE" NICKS HAD BEEN brought up primarily in Phoenix, Arizona, and Los Angeles, but her family moved around some as her father climbed up the corporate ladder of the Armour and Greyhound firms. Like Buckingham, she had started early with music, singing with her grandfather as a child and writing songs of bitter teenage heartbreak at age 16. Songwriting developed into her passion, and by now her prodigious output far exceeds the songs that Fleetwood Mac actually puts on record. She has recorded demos regularly—"Leather and Lace," sung with the Eagles' Don Henley (at one time a rumored Nicks boyfriend), is just one of the good ones languishing in some tape box—and while stories of Helen Reddy recording a Stevie original are as yet without evidence, she has had some songs covered and hopes to have more. "It's not like I need something else to do," she admitted to *Record World*, after mentioning that she may record in a solo format. "But there's no way Fleetwood Mac can do all my songs, and I've got a library of songs I want to be done. Some of them could be done by me, some by somebody else, and some can be done by Fleetwood Mac."

Stevie Nicks.

After three years in Fleetwood Mac, Stevie is the group's star attraction. But she's by no means using the band as simply a steppingstone to a solo career; recently, when they were given yet another Don Kirshner Rock Award, this one in the absurd category of "Best Rock Personalities," Nicks accepted, saying, "We've never thought of ourselves as personalities. We're just a band."

Nor does Stevie particularly seek the limelight. While on tour, she tends to keep to herself and a couple of friends who accompany her, looking after her fragile health; and even if she may be a little less accessible to the public and press than Mick or the others, in conversation she is talkative, confiding, friendly. This band is not Fleetwood Mac, featuring Stevie Nicks. It is Fleetwood Mac, five different individuals forming one extraordinary unit.

WHILE BUCKINGHAM AND NICKS HAD met briefly during high school, it wasn't until they were in college that they began to play music together regularly. Lindsey had joined a band called Fritz, and Stevie was asked to join as well, "because we knew she was a singer." Once the band had gotten rolling, Buckingham had taken up electric guitar as well as acoustic, "but when we got into a more acid-rock sound," he recalls, "I switched to bass and we got a guitarist who could play screaming leads."

Fritz proved to be a worthy enough investment for its members to quit school and migrate south from the Bay Area, where the band had formed, to Los Angeles. They encountered plenty of problems, though, peddling what Buckingham calls "San Francisco rock, kind of quasi-jazz with lots of involved changes." He and Nicks had "started seeing each other romantically," and "around 1971" they left Fritz together. Lindsey immediately contracted a year-long case of mononucleosis, but he resumed guitar playing, and with the aid of his trusty four-track tape recorder they worked diligently on their own songs. They met Keith Olsen, the engineer, and one thing led to another: in 1972 (the year Fleetwood Mac made *Bare Trees*) they recorded an album for the Polydor label.

Given the tidal wave of records released every year, literally thousands of them, it's no surprise that several good ones are swallowed in the undertow. *Buckingham Nicks* was such an album: not a block-buster, but one that certainly deserved more attention than it got.

Songs were by Buckingham and/or Nicks, with the exception of an acoustic guitar rendition of "Django," an instrumental by pianist John Lewis of the Modern Jazz Quartet. Danny Kirwan had also admired the legendary gypsy guitarist Django Reinhardt; in fact, Buckingham and Kirwan in many ways shared the same musical approach. They both were craftsmen, building layers of guitar tracks into a textural whole. Just as Welch described Kirwan (and even as Welch was himself), Stevie Nicks says that "Lindsey knew exactly what he wanted to do in the studio." Each was more in his element when recording than when on stage, although Buckingham has since become a powerful live performer; and each worked out his material thoroughly before waxing it. Lindsey himself recognizes his prowess in the studio: soon after Fleetwood Mac's *Rumours* was released, he remarked that "I think that if there's any sort of

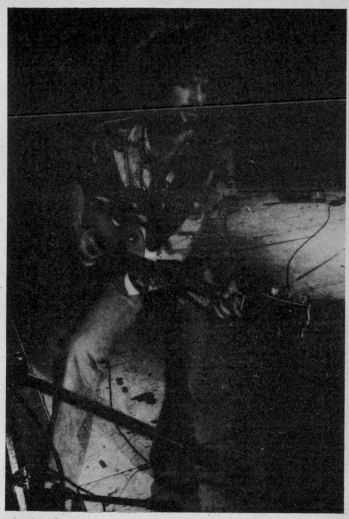

Lindsey Buckingham.

unique talent that I have, it's just being able to do what a producer does in the studio."

Buckingham's acoustic guitar work was one of the things that made *Buckingham Nicks* so attractive. They knew how to rock—he had absorbed plenty of those old '50s records—but the insistent rock pulse was always painted with the soothing colors of clearly produced acoustic guitars. To be sure, there was no ignoring electricity (as in "Don't Let Me Down Again," which was rock and roll with the accent on the roll, and would have sounded even better with Fleetwood on drums), but it was used mainly as another color. On both "Races Are Run" and "Frozen Love," for instance, the acoustic-electric interplay was remarkable in its variety of tonal shadings.

Buckingham Nicks was not without its problems, foremost among which were the lyrics. Nicks, though skilled at combining chords and melody, tended to get mired in vapid, late '60s hippie poetics ("Sunflowers and your face fascinate me/You go into the dusty pink day"), over-reliance on simile ("And the water was closing all around like a glove") or just plain redundancy ("Do you always trust your first initial feeling?") when it came to the words. What's more, her singing could be almost too emotive, too drawn out. But these were weak links that maturity and experience couldn't help but strengthen. She was clearly a vocalist with power and feel, and Buckingham's brighter, rather high tones gave them an enviable one-two punch, with two capable soloists who could also sing together, not only in harmony ("Crystal") but in counterpoint ("Frozen Love").

Buckingham Nicks did not do well, which naturally was a blow. As Buckingham says, "We didn't know it was standard procedure for a company to throw a lot of albums out on the market and not push any of them, hoping that maybe one or two would be hits. At 23 or so, we had no idea of hard realities."

A major problem other than record company backing was getting gigs to support the album. They had no touring band, so they couldn't even perform it the way it was recorded. For some mysterious reason, though, the folks in Birmingham, Alabama picked up heavily on the record, and they did several concerts there using old Fritz pals and others for a band. Playing for 7,000 people in Dixie "really blew our minds," Lindsey recalls. "I mean, going from being nobody in L.A. to being big stars in Birmingham—it was ridiculous."

Gigs in Birmingham weren't exactly a regularity, and record royalties never materialized, so Nicks had long since taken a waitress job in Hollywood when Mick Fleetwood called. They were destitute—Lindsey had no job at all—but they had begun work on another record at Sound City, hoping to sell it after completion. Hence the inital reluctance to abandon Buckingham Nicks and join Fleetwood Mac, a reluctance that was compounded by a basic lack of familiarity with the Mac's previous work.

Stevie Nicks: "I knew... I knew that, ah... To be perfectly honest, I didn't know a whole lot about Fleetwood Mac. I knew they had to be somebody big and they had a girl singer. I remembered hearing Christine sing 'Show Me a Smile' on TV, and I thought it was really nice she was in the band.

"Even without knowing much about them, I was awestruck. The night Keith told us that Mick might ask us to join, this friend of ours who was really into Fleetwood Mac was there. He told us about seeing them at Winterland and how they'd driven away in big black Cadillac limousines. So there I was in Clementine's outfit and white nurse's shoes, going 'Oh my God!' and imagining those limos. I think that was the only time I've ever been really awestruck about this whole thing, seeing that picture in my head.''

Buckingham recalls that joining Fleetwood Mac was a casual, easy process: "As soon as we all met together there was a definite rapport, and we just said 'Yeah, OK!' and that was that.'' Since another album was scheduled immediately, they rehearsed it and recorded it before ever appearing together on stage.

Fleetwood Mac.

MORE THAN TWO YEARS HAD PASSED since *Buckingham Nicks*, and it had done them good. Stevie had gotten control over what she wanted to express. Her voice became just raw enough when it needed to be, sensual when she wanted it to be, but rarely overbearing. She had also honed her songwriting chops; and the solid Fleetwood-McVie rhythm section was exactly what her songs called for.

"Rhiannon" was the real triumph. With Fleetwood directing the flow, it fell into an easy but hypnotic groove, building a simple chord pattern with understated power. Splashes of guitar and backing vocals came in at just the right times, always in support of Nicks' lead, while John McVie's bass wound its way gracefully through. Stevie's lyrics about a Welsh witch were among her best:

> She is like a cat in the dark
> And then she is the darkness
> She rules her life like a fine skylark
> And when the sky is starless...

"Crystal," Nicks' tune from the earlier album, made a reappearance, and an already nice song was helped considerably by Chris McVie's wandering organ lines. "Landslide," another Nicks contribution, was a soft acoustic number that she now dedicates to each of the band's audiences. Each of Stevie's songs had its own character, its own appeal.

The same could be said for Lindsey Buckingham's material; in fact, it was apparent right away that this new Fleetwood Mac could handle a lot of different styles, all of them naturally, and still keep the music within easy reach of anyone. Lindsey's "Monday Morning" opened the album with a dose of the '50s influence, a little like Buddy Holly but harder. The tasty slide guitar solo was typical of the maturity of his playing. He'd obviously been playing plenty of electric, and now gave it equal billing (or more) with acoustic. Solos were just right for each song's mood, and virtuosity took second place to *feel*.

Buckingham rocked out again on "Blue Letter"—written by the Curtis Brothers, the one non-original on the album—again very forceful and driving. The majestic "I'm So Afraid" was reminiscent of the *Buckingham Nicks* days, with the same full production, while "World Turning" was essentially a bluesy guitar riff with equally bluesy singing by Chris and Lindsey, a malleable tune that grew out of experimenting in the studio. Fleetwood added some African talking drum to the latter, and on tour it became his percussion showpiece.

Christine, with her own style firmly established since *Penguin*, didn't pull any punches on *Fleetwood Mac*. There was no reason for her to do anything other than what she did best—easy-rocking love songs—especially when she did it so damn well. "Warm Ways" and "Over My Head" were especially nice. The first was as soft as its title, with Buckingham adding some wistful, Kirwanesque solo guitar. The second was like a wide, soothing wave, with the listener swept up in its current.

It took them by surprise when "Over My Head" became the first single, as Christine remembers it: "It was the last track we kept, and we really didn't know what we were going to do with it. All it had was a vocal, a dobro guitar and a drum track—we weren't sure what to add to that. So I put on a little Vox Continental organ and Lindsey added some electric guitar, and it developed this really pleasant atmosphere.

It didn't batter you. But it was the last track we ever thought would be a single."

This then was the album that would pick up momentum from its release in late 1975 all through the following year and a half, languishing for 70 or 80 weeks in the lofty reaches of all the charts and racking up phenomenal sales (more than two years after its release, Warners still reports sales of 50,000 copies every week). But it wasn't greeted with dancing in the streets of Burbank at the time. Actually, after the *Heroes* disappointment and with the Davis gloom still lingering, attitudes were pretty ho-hum at Warner Bros. What's more, the master tapes of the album were misplaced at one point, only to be found in a pile of material doomed for erasure!

Don Schmitzerle, a former Warners executive now with Capricorn Records, represented one of the more positive attitudes: "There was always an underlying confidence in the band—we never gave a thought to not picking up their option [renewing their contract]. We felt the group was inevitable, by virtue of surviving so many changes and continuing to sell their 250,000 albums. They were the most resilient group I ever knew; but we couldn't seem to get beyond that 250,000, constantly selling to the same people." And while Schmitzerle contends that he and others were genuinely excited about *Fleetwood Mac*—"We felt something we had never felt before, a genuine energy"—he admits that "the company's attitude wasn't nearly in proportion to selling three million

John McVie.

Christine McVie.

albums. We didn't want to get our expectations way up."

With the help of promo man Paul Ahern (who more recently worked minor miracles as manager of the group Boston), "Over My Head" began to get a lot of radio airplay in important "secondary markets," smaller cities whose radio activity is vital in breaking a record. "Once we got a representative number of secondaries playing it," says Schmitzerle, "we put together a $25,000 AM radio campaign, using 'Over My Head' as a bed for the commercials." The eventual results are well known by now, with three successful singles coming from the one album.

ONCE AGAIN FLEETWOOD MAC HAD CREDibility as a singles band, for the first time since the brilliant string of Peter Green-led 45's in England, and the hits definitely played a role in the group's explosion. The wide variety offered on the album—blues-rock to soft-rock to straight ballad, all of it very palatable—was also a big plus. But there were other factors as well, and the descriptions of band members past and present shed some light on just what those factors were and are.

As Chris McVie puts it, "We have a situation now that's a little bit different, because quite by accident in our search for members of the band we happen to have run across a very unique formula that happens to be commercial, while retaining the quality of other Fleetwood Macs. And it happened without our doing anything that was sacrilegious to our tastes."

John McVie: "This band seems to cover things from every angle: there are three strong writers, three good singers, plus a well-established and, I hope, well-respected name. And it seems the time was right for a rock band with two girl singers—a real *rock* band, not like the New Seekers or ABBA, where the girls act as if they'd never seen a Tampax in their lives."

Bob Welch, who has had a long time to ponder his departure and remains convinced he made the right move, has some further insight into the current group's appeal: "When I was with Fleetwood I felt above the audience, as if I knew something they didn't know. If they feel that vibe coming from you, they get hesitant. What people want to see in a big commercial success is a reflection of what they themselves could be, a nicer, prettier version of themselves. When I was in the band we were distant, and people weren't comfortable. Now they are.

"I think people wondered about *Bare Trees* or *Mystery To Me* songs—y'know, 'What's that all about?'— but now Lindsey is singing, 'Monday Morning I want to squeeze you in the crotch,' and it's easy to identify with. They're a recognizable band. Instead of the weird, underground image we had before, the image is basically one of nice kids from the Valley. And they're definitely not an English band anymore. They're not obscure or bizarre—they're a California band."

Stevie Nicks: "One of the big things was that we went right out on the road, so we not only had a new album but a live show. We played constantly, and everywhere, places like Casper, Wyoming and Normal, Illinois. And people were so wonderful and gave us such good vibes that you just knew we sold tons of albums every time we played.

Stevie Nicks and Christine McVie.

"Everybody is so different from everybody else. Look at us on stage: we don't even look like we're going to the same place. We know we're not virtuosos. We're very loose on stage, but I think the audience picks up that we're having a really good time up there. At some point during almost every set I'm laughing so hard I can barely continue, mostly because of Mick."

The live show was unquestionably one of the keys to Fleetwood Mac's resurgence.

The value of three different singers and writers was not only aural but visual, with the audience given a constantly shifting focal point. Not since the era of Green-Kirwan-Spencer had they offered such a strong front line. And just as the earlier band had been (except Kirwan), they were at their best on stage. John McVie still thrived on the road as much as when he played sweat-soaked, matchbox-sized clubs in London ten years back, and Christine was a natural with plenty of her own experience. Fleetwood habitually shed his practical off-stage posture and became the embodiment of the slightly daft Englishman, leering madly as he pounded away. Buckingham took some time to relax in performance, but he gained confidence with every gig on the endless tours. Performing was (and is) the basic way they related to their fans; as Nicks said, they sold albums because of concerts, not vice versa.

In Stevie Nicks Fleetwood Mac had its first really vibrant performer since Green and Spencer had left. Her "Rhiannon" developed into a febrile show stopper, "a very different kettle of fish than the one on record," as Chris McVie describes it. "It created a huge impact on stage, with little Stevie floating around in her black chiffon and top hat—people got really excited about it. And she's a very natural performer."

Nicks recalled for *Record World* the effect that a Janis Joplin performance had on her when Fritz happened to open a show for Joplin in Santa Clara, California: "...She walked on stage, and for an hour and a half, Stevie's chin was on the floor: I mean, you couldn't have pried me away with a million dollar check. I was absolutely glued to her, and there is where I learned a lot of what I do on stage. It wasn't that I wanted to be like her, because I didn't. But I said, 'If ever I am a performer of any value, I want to be able to create the same kind of feeling that's going on between her and her audience.'" Stevie's on stage feeling became one of grace and vulnerability. Like Chris McVie, she forged a bond of intimacy with people, but in a very different way. Stevie was more demonstrative, more direct in her appeals, and the audience soon re-

Stevie Nicks.

sponded in kind, reacting to her every gesture with noisy affection.

SOME UNWANTED PUBLICITY—CAUSED IN part by the band's own candor—surrounded the romantic splits involving Fleetwood Mac members. Mick and Jenny Fleetwood's volatile relationship had survived the Bob Weston incident, as well as some other problems. But Mick's increasing responsibilities as band manager had drawn them apart, and they were divorced in the spring of 1976. However, not long after that they again moved in together, and they re-married on October 1 of that same year.

Most of the attention was focused on the McVie/McVie and Buckingham/Nicks splits They weren't so unusual in themselves—like most breakups, they were painful, gradual and often irrational—but it was unique simply to have two couples in one rock band, let alone two couples on the rocks.

The McVies were married in 1968, and they were together constantly in Fleetwood Mac from 1970 on. John's liquor intake sometimes gave him a Jekyll and Hyde personality, sober and friendly by day but drunk and belligerent by night, which couldn't have helped matters. But mainly, after six years of uninterrupted gigging and recording, they needed to be apart. As for Stevie and Lindsey, Stevie admits that "Lindsey's and my relationship was rocky when we joined, and it certainly didn't get any better."

Living and working with one's spouse inevitably had to take its toll. "Suppose Lindsey wasn't playing well on a particular song or something," Nicks suggests. "As a girlfriend, I should be a comfort: you know,

Lindsey Buckingham, John McVie and Mick Fleetwood.

'Who cares, you're great.' I mean, that's what old ladies do, right? But I couldn't, because I was one-fifth of the people who were saying. 'Look, if you could just get your guitar part right, then we could put the vocal on.' So we couldn't get any comfort at all from each other about what went on in the band. There was no love—everyone was too nervous. And while we were traveling all the time, none of us had other friends to talk to. I think Lindsey and I talk more now than we ever did.''

Nicks' last comment is typical of their present-day frames of mind. They stuck it out and kept the band together because they knew, corny as it sounds, that they had had a good thing going musically, good enough to preserve over their personal problems. It's true that they were also raking in the bucks. Cynicism aside, though, one feels that that was hardly their only motivation for enduring.

Mick Fleetwood and pliers.

Christine McVie, John McVie, Mick Fleetwood, Stevie Nicks, Lindsey Buckingham.

FLEETWOOD MAC BEGAN ITS LATEST album, *Rumours*, around February, 1976. It would take close to a year to finish, partly due to the continuing romantic withdrawals and also because "we kind of got off to a slow start on it," says Buckingham. "Everybody was burned out after so much touring, and we really should have been taking a vacation."

Rumours was also a long time coming because it was made with more care than the new band's first album. During the *Fleetwood Mac* sessions they hardly knew each other—each writer brought in a finished song and it was recorded. But all the touring had pulled them into a unit. This time they were able to experiment in the studio, each person contributing to each song. And the care that was taken with *Rumours* extended to co-producers Richard Dashut and Ken

Caillat's personally supervising every tedious step, from synchronizing vocals and instrumental tracks on separate tape machines to cutting the "master" discs and making cassettes from the masters. As a result, the sound of the album was superb.

With *Fleetwood Mac's* success, they found themselves in what was for them an extraordinary position. The people at Warner Bros. were excited about the new album, holding exhaustive meetings about every aspect of marketing their new stars and committing their money and staff, in force, to making *Rumours* every bit as successful. Out in consumerland, a great deal more than the hard-core fans found themselves eagerly looking forward to *Rumours'* imminent release. Disc jockeys raved about the new single, "Go Your Own Way." Warners reported that the initial shipment of 800,000 units of the album was the largest in the company's history. Fleetwood Mac became a big deal.

Speculation was rife as to how the romance would affect the music. Would Nicks' love songs be thinly disguised odes to Don Henley and the Jefferson Starship's Paul Kantner (another supposed boyfriend, post-Lindsey)? Would there be muffled sounds of furniture breaking as the McVies went at each other in the studio, as the Rona Barretts of rock hoped? Would it be, as McVie himself said, "Mary Hartman on wax?"

Stevie Nicks: "The heartache definitely affected the music, but in a very excellent way. The new album has more substance, because there was more to write about. I think anybody will be able to listen to this record and say, 'Well, there it is. That's what happened during two years.'"

When *Rumours* finally came out, the splits were very apparent. Buckingham's outlook progressed from the initial reactions of "Second Hand News" ("I know there's nothing to say/Someone has taken my place") to the bitter "Go Your Own Way" ("Shacking up is all you wanna do") and the resigned "Never Going Back Again" ("Been down one time/Been down two times/I'm never going back again"). Nicks countered with "Dreams" ("Now here you go again/You say you want your Freedom") and "Silver Springs," a song held from the album but put on the "B side" of the first single, in which she sang about an affair on the road ("Don't say that she's pretty/And did you say that she loyed you/Baby, I don't want to know"). Chris McVie, perhaps the best at putting things in perspective, showed that she would rather celebrate new love ("Songbird," "You Make Loving Fun") than mourn old. But what was most apparent was that *Rumours* came from the cooperation of five people, with a new tightness embodied by such things as the full and confident backing vocals. The haunting "The Chain," a bit of editing wizardry sown by everyone from the seeds of several different songs—and their first five-person publishing credit—was one of their most ambitious tracks ever.

Lindsey Buckingham came into his own. His "Second Hand News" opened the album much as "Monday Morning" opened *Fleetwood Mac*, with a touch of Buddy Holly on the hard stuff. Those who thought the latter tune should have been a hit single were more than satisfied by "Go Your Own Way," a track so hot it made you sweat just thinking about it; the combination of Buckingham's jangling twelve-string acoustic and wailing electric were his best balance of the two yet. For straight acoustic fans, the music-box picking of "Never Going Back Again" was delightful. Much like George Harrison with the Beatles, Lindsey developed a sense of what each of his parts required in order to fit the context of the song.

Christine McVie continued to mine her vein of consistently accessible love songs. "Don't Stop," which paired her with Buckingham on the lead vocal, continued in the rollicking style first heard on "Dissatisfied," from Penguin. "You Make Loving Fun" cooked like crazy while matching a lilting chorus with angelic backing vocals. Her two ballads, "Oh Daddy" and "Songbird," were lovely and expressive. And McVie also showed that as an instrumentalist, she knows just what should go where: her organ on "Dreams," clavinet on "You Make Loving Fun" and piano on "Don't Stop" revealed an intuitive feel for texture.

Stevie Nicks completed what was once again a something-for-everyone appeal. "Dreams" and "Gold Dust Woman" preserved the hypnotic drive that made "Rhiannon" such a winner, and both have easily become similar concert tours de force; with "Dreams" alone Stevie proved herself a songwriter to be reckoned with, if she wasn't already recognized as such.

NO QUESTION ABOUT IT: RUMOURS WAS A sure shot from the day it was released. It wasn't long before those first 800,000 copies were sold—Rumours didn't have to pick up momentum, as Fleetwood Mac did, because the group had established itself as a superstar act. Within a few weeks after its release, helped along by immediate and extensive radio airplay on both AM and FM stations and the attendant sales (which were incredible, despite a $7.98 suggested list price), it climbed into the top position on the *Record World*, *Billboard* and *Cash Box* charts, remaining there in each case for well over twenty weeks; in fact, it dropped out of *Billboard's* #1 slot after twenty-nine weeks, and in *Record World* it stayed at #1 for well over thirty weeks consecutively. Warner Bros. was expecting to realize sales of some eight million copies of *Rumours* by Christmas, 1977, and nearly a year after it came out it was still selling briskly at 200,000 copies each week, according to the record company. At that rate, it stood a solid chance of overtaking the biggest pop albums of all time, Carole King's *Tapestry* and Peter Frampton's *Comes Alive*. There was precious little competition for top seller of 1977 honors.

To be sure, *Rumours'* overwhelming reception by the public could in part be explained by the overall good health of the record industry in a time when "platinum" albums (indicating sales of one million units) are relatively common. But there was much more. For one thing, the album proved to be a bottomless well of hit singles. "Go Your Own Way" was followed by the sultry "Dreams," which became their first American #1 single; "Dreams" was soon followed by "Don't Stop," then by "You Make Loving Fun," and all of them made the top ten. And even after four hits from one album, there was a strong potential for more, with "Second Hand News" and "The Chain" among the likely candidates. Canny marketing techniques on the part of Warners were undoubtedly instrumental in the string of hits, but in the long run no amount of superior business acumen can carry a record if the quality of the music is lacking. With *Rumours* it definitely was not.

Millions of albums aren't sold simply on the basis of airplay and hearsay. Concerts are absolutely vital for

John McVie, Lindsey Buckingham, Mick Fleetwood, Christine McVie, Stevie Nicks.

stimulating sales, and the unveiling of *Rumours* was followed in short order by the most extensive tour Fleetwood Mac has yet undertaken. Beginning in March, 1977 and taking only occasional breaks, they traveled not only across the U.S. but to Europe, Japan, Australia and New Zealand as well. The demand for tickets during this tour affirmed their status as pop music's top attraction; in Los Angeles, for instance, they sold out three straight nights at the 18,000 seat Forum and could likely have pitched their tents in that venue for a week or more. And the more they played, the stronger their concert presentation got. After settling on a basic set drawn almost entirely from *Rumours* and *Fleetwood Mac* ("Oh Well" was the only oldie), they honed their performance into a versatile, well paced showcase aggressively displaying all of their talents. Even Stevie's nagging

Mick Fleetwood, Stevie Nicks, John McVie, Christine McVie, Lindsey Buckingham.

throat problems—the cause of several cancellations, including some three weeks of gigs at the outset of the tour—didn't prevent them from logging close to one hundred appearances. This is a band that likes to work, and in 1977 their eagerness to make themselves available to the public paid some handsome dividends, both musically and financially.

RUMOURS PROVED THAT FLEETWOOD MAC was no fluke. The kudos for this record have been legion. Not only has it been universally recognized as 1977's top seller, it has received critical acclaim to match. And the future looks very bright indeed. Two albums, after all, are hardly going to exhaust the group's potential, and even if Buckingham and Chris McVie are only half as prolific as Nicks in the songwriting department, their well of good but as yet unused material must be very deep.

But suppose—just suppose—that something should happen to break up this line-up. Stevie Nicks, for one, has admitted that the demands of the road may eventually force her to quit, while Lindsey, cognizant of his prowess in the studio, may turn to production work somewhere down the line. These are hardly inevitabilites—on the contrary, at this point they are barely possibilities—but one wonders nevertheless. Would Fleetwood and the McVies, after their biggest success, recruit new members and continue the Fleetwood Mac name?

Christine McVie: "Undoubtedly. John and Mick and I are each other's driving forces. People that we add on are our inspiration and our vital support, but they're not indispensable. We've always just found the right combination, never searching for a specific sound, just by accident.

"Mick has so much energy—he's a pile-driver. I have a lot of faith in him. He might be the real driving force, but John's like a sleeping partner, a sidekick who's always there. As for myself, I'd never want to be in another band, playing with anyone else."

John McVie: "The object of this band has never been, 'OK, let's get these people in the band and record these songs so we can make lots of money and I can go sit on my yacht and not have to work for another year.' If the next album is a stiff, you don't just go out and become a plumber. You keep playing, because that's what you do. You always hope it will last indefinitely, but right at the back of your mind you know that somewhere along the line someone's gonna go, 'Listen, I've got to do something different.' You always try not to think about that. But the band would still go on, until it comes to the point where

Mick or myself just don't want to do it any more—which unfortunately will happen in the far distant future."

Here's hoping it's the far, *far* distant future.

The three writers; Christine McVie, Lindsey Buckingham and Stevie Nicks.

Mick Fleetwood and John McVie, "Seedy Management."

The Original Fleetwood Mac Album (back cover).

FLEETWOOD MAC DISCOGRAPHY

(compiled by Greg Shaw)

(E)-English release (A) = American

MICK FLEETWOOD BEFORE FLEETWOOD MAC (with The Cheynes)

12-63   Respectable/It's Gonna Happen To You—Columbia 7153 (E)

10-64   Goin' to the River/Cheyne-Re-La—Columbia 7386 (E)

2-65   Down and Out/Stop Running Around—Columbia 7464 (E)

(with the Bo Street Runners)

7-65   Baby Never Say Goodbye/Get Out of My Way—Columbia 7640 (E)

(with Peter B's Looners)

3-66   If You Wanna Be Happy/Jodrell Blues—Columbia 7862 (E)

(with Shotgun Express)

10-66   I Could Feel the Whole World Turn Round/Curtains—Columbia 8025 (E)

2-67   Funny, Neither Could I/Indian Thing—Columbia 8178 (E)

(with John Mayall's Bluesbreakers)

5-67   Double Trouble/It Hurts Me Too—Decca 12621 (E)

PETER GREEN BEFORE FLEETWOOD MAC

(with Peter B's Looners)

3-66   If You Wanna Be Happy/Jodrell Blues—Columbia 7862(E)

(with Shotgun Express)

10-66   I Could Feel the Whole World Turn Round/Curtains—Columbia 8025(E)

2-67   Funny, Neither Could I/Indian Thing—Columbia 8178 (E)

(with John Mayall's Bluesbreakers)

10-66   Looking Back/So Many Roads—Decca 12506(E)

11-66   Sitting in the Rain/Out of Reach—Decca 12545(E)

3-67   Curly/Rubber Duck—Decca 12588(E)

5-67   Double Trouble/It Hurts Me Too—Decca 12621(E)

2-67   EP: John Mayall's Bluesbreakers with Paul Butterfield—Decca 8673(E)

3-67   *A Hard Road*—Decca 4853(E)/London 502(A)
A Hard Road/It's Over/You Don't Love Me/The Stumble/Another Kinda Love/Hit the Highway/Leaping Christine/Dust My Blues/There's Always Work/The Same Way/The Supernatural/Top of the Hill/Someday After Awhile(You'll Be Sorry)/Living Alone

4-67   *Raw Blues* (various artists)—Decca Ace of Clubs 1220(E)Evil Woman Blues

5-67   *Eddie Boyd and His Blues Band* (featuring Peter Green)—Decca 4872(E)
Too Bad Pt. 1/Dust My Broom/Unfair Lovers/Key to the Highway/Vacation from the Blues/Steak

House/Letter Missin' Blues/Ain't Doin' Too
Bad/Blue Coast Man/The Train is Coming/Save
Her Doctor/Rack 'em Back/Too Bad Pt. 2/The
Big Bell/Pinetop's Boogie Woogie/Night Time is
the Right Time

JOHN McVIE BEFORE FLEETWOOD MAC

(with John Mayall's Bluesbreakers)

4-64   Crawling Up a Hill/Mr. James—Decca 11900(E)

4-65   Crocodile Walk/Blues City Shakedown—Decca
         12120(E)

10-65   I'm Your Witchdoctor/Telephone Blues—Imme-
         diate 012(E)/Immediate 502 (A)

11-65   Loney Years/Bernard Jenkins—Purdah(E)

8-66   Parchman Farm/Key to Love—Decca 12490(E)/
         London 20016(A)

10-66   Looking Back/So Many Roads—Decca 12506(E)

12-66   Sitting in the Rain/Out of Reach—Decca
         12545(E)

3-67   Curly/Rubber Duck—Decca 12588(E)/London
         20039 (A)

5-67   Double Trouble/It Hurts Me Too—Decca 12621

2-67   EP:John Mayall's Bluesbreakers with Paul But-
         terfield—Decca 8673(E)

2-65   *John Mayall Plays John Mayall*—Decca 4680
         Crawling Up a Hill/I Wanna Teach You Every-
         thing/When I'm Gone/I Need Your Love/The
         Hoot Owl/R&B Time/Night Train/Lucille Croco-
         dile Walk/What's the Matter with You/Doreen/
         Runaway/Heartache/Chicago Line

3-66   *Blues Breakers*—Decca 4804(E)/London 492 (A)
         All Your Love/Hideaway/Little Girl/Another
         Man/Double Crossing Time/What'd I Say/Key
         to Love/Parchman Farm/Have Your Heard/
         Ramblin' On My Mind/Steppin' Out/It Ain't
         Right

1-67   *A Hard Road*—Decca 4853(E)/London 502(A)
         (details above)

159

5-67   *Eddie Boyd and His Blues Band* (featuring Peter Green)—Decca 4872(E)
(details above)

7-67   Crusade—Decca 4890(E)/London 529(A)
Oh Pretty Woman/Stand Back Baby/My Time After Awhile/Snowy Wood/Man of Stone/Tears in My Eyes/Driving Sideways/The Death of J.B. Lenoir/I Can't Quit You Baby/Streamline/Me and My Woman/Checking On My Baby

CHRISTINE PERFECT (McVIE) BEFORE FLEETWOOD MAC

(with Chicken Shack)

12-67   It's Okay With Me Baby/When My Left Eye Jumps—Blue Horizon 3135(E)

9-68   Worried About My Woman/Six Nights in Seven—Blue Horizon 3145(E)/Epic 10414(A)

12-68   When the Train Comes Back/Hey Baby—Blue Horizon 3146(E)

4-69   I'd Rather Go Blind/Night Life—Blue Horizon 3153(E)

9-69   Tears in the Wind/Things You Put Me Through—Blue Horizon 100(A)

7-68   *Forty Blue Fingers Freshly Packed and Ready to Serve*—Blue Horizon 63203(E)/Epic 26414(A)
Letter/Lonesome Whistle Blues/When the Train Comes Back/San-Ho-Zay/King of the World/See Me Baby/First Time I Met the Blues/Webbed Feet/You Ain't No Good/What You Did Last Night

O.K. Ken—Blue Horizon 63209(E)/Blue Horizon 7705(A)
Baby's Got Me Crying/Right Way Is My Way/Get Like You Used to Be/Pony and Trap/Tell Me/Woman is the Blues/I Wanna See My Baby/Remington Ride/Fishing in your River/Mean Old World/Sweet Sixteen

(as Christine Perfect)

6-69   I'd Rather Go Blind/Close to Me—Blue Horizon 300(A)

8-69   I'd Rather Go Blind/Get Like You Used to Be—Epic 10536(A)

10-69   When You Say/No Road Is the Right Road—Blue Horizon 3165(E)

4-70   I'm Too Far Gone/Close to Me—Blue Horizon 3172(E)

10-69   *Christine Perfect*—Blue Horizon 63860(E)
Crazy 'Bout You Baby/I'm On My Way/Let Me Go/Wait and See/Close to Me/I'd Rather Go Blind/When You Say/And That's Saying a Lot/No Road Is the Right Road/For You/I'm Too Far Gone/I Want You

8-76   *The Legendary Christine Perfect Album*—Sire 6022(A)(reissue of above)

BUCKINGHAM & NICKS BEFORE FLEETWOOD MAC

6-73   *Buckingham Nicks*—Polydor 5058(A)
Don't Let Me Down Again/Long Distance Winner/Crying in the Night/Without a Leg to Stand on/Crystal/Races are Run/Lola (My Love)/Frozen Love/Stephanie/Django

FLEETWOOD MAC SINGLES

1967   I Believe My Time Ain't Long/Rambling Pony—Blue Horizon 3051(E)

1968   Black Magic Woman/The Sun is Shining—Blue Horizon 57-3138(E)

1968   Black Magic Woman/Long Gray Mare—Epic 10351(A)

1968   Need Your Love So Bad/Stop Messin' Round—Blue Horizon 57-3139(E)/Epic 10386(A)

1968   Albatross/Jigsaw Puzzle Blues—Blue Horizon 57-3145(E)/Epic 10436(A)

1969   Man of the World/Somebody's Gonna Get Their Head Kicked In Tonite—Immediate 080(E)

1969   Rattlesnake Shake/Coming Your Way—Reprise 0860(A)

1969   Oh Well Pt.1/Pt.2—Reprise 27000(E)/Reprise 0883(A)

1970   The Green Manalishi/World in Harmony—Reprise 27007(E)Reprise 0925(A)

1970	Jewel Eyed Judy/Station Man—Reprise 0984 (A)
1971	Sands of Time/Lay It All Down—Reprise 1057 (A)
1971	Dragonfly/Purple Dancer—Reprise 27010 (E)
1972	Oh Well Pt. 1/The Green Manalishi—Reprise 1079 (A)
1972	Albatross/Jigsaw Puzzle Blues—Blue Horizon 3145 (E)
1972	Sentimental Lady/Sunny Side of Heaven—Reprise 1093 (A)
1973	Albatross/Need Your Love So Bad—CBS 8306 (E)
1973	Remember Me/Dissatisfied—Reprise 1159 (A)
1973	Revelation/Did You Ever Love Me—Reprise 1172 (A)
1973	Did You Ever Love Me/Derelict—Warner 14280 (E)
1973	Black Magic Woman/Stop Messin' Around—CBS 1722 (E)
1974	For Your Love/Hypnotized—Reprise 14315 (E)/Reprise 1188 (A)
1974	Heroes Are Hard to Find/Born Enchanter—Reprise 14388 (E)/Reprise 1317 (A)
1975	Warm Ways/Blue Letter—Reprise 14403 (E)
1975	Over My Head/I'm So Afraid—Reprise 14413 (E)/Reprise 1339 (A)
1976	Rhiannon/Sugar Daddy—Reprise 14430 (E)/Reprise 1345 (A)
1976	Albatross/Black Magic Woman—Epic 11029 (A)
1976	Say You Love Me/Monday Morning—Reprise 14447 (E)/Reprise 1356 (A)
1976	Go Your Own Way/Silver Springs—Warner Bros. 8304 (A)
1977	Don't Stop/Never Going Back Again—Warner Bros. 8413 (A)

1977   Dreams/Songbird—Warner Bros. 8371 (A)

1977   You Make Loving Fun/Gold Dust Woman—
        Warner Bros. 8483 (A)

FLEETWOOD MAC ALBUMS

2-68   *Peter Green's Fleetwood Mac*—Blue Horizon
        63200 (E)/Epic 26402 (A)
        My Heart Beat Like a Hammer/Merry Go
        Round/Long Grey Mare/Hellhound on My
        Trail/Shake Your Moneymaker/Looking for
        Somebody/No Place to Go/My Baby's Good to
        Me/I Loved Another Woman/Cold Black Night/
        The World Keep On Turning/Got to Move

11-68   *Mr. Wonderful*—Blue Horizon 63205 (E)
        Stop Messin' Round/Coming Home/Rollin'
        Man/Dust My Broom/Love That Burns/Doctor
        Brown/Need Your Love Tonight/If You Be My
        Baby/Evenin' Boogie/Lazy Poker Blues/I've
        Lost My Baby/Trying So Hard to Forget

1-69   *English Rose*—Epic 26446 (A) (reissued on Co-
        lumbia Special Products P 11651)
        Stop Messin' Round/Jigsaw Puzzle Blues/Doctor
        Brown/Something Inside of Me/Evening Boo-
        gie/Love That Burns/Black Magic Woman/I've
        Lost My Baby/One Sunny Day/Without You/
        Coming Home/Albatross

3-69   *The Pious Bird of Good Omen*—Blue Horizon
        63215 (E) (compilation)
        Need Your Love So Bad/Coming Home/Ram-
        bling Pony/The Big Boat/I Believe My Time Ain't
        Long/The Sun Is Shining/Albatross/Just the
        Blues/Jigsaw Puzzle Blues/Looking for Some-
        body/Stop Messin' Round

10-69   *Then Play On*—Reprise 6368 (A)/Reprise 9000 (E)
        (reissued as Warner 44103)
        Coming Your Way/Closing My Eyes/Fighting
        for Madge/When You Say/Show-Biz Blues/Un-
        derway/Although the Sun is Shining/Rattle-
        snake Shake/Searching for Madge/My Dream/
        Like Crying/Before the Beginning (later
        re-released with "Oh Well" replacing "When
        You Say" and "My Dream" in the U.S.)

2-70   *Blues Jam in Chicago, Vol. 1*—Blue Horizon 4803
(A)
Watch Out/Ooh Baby/South Indiana, Take 1/
South Indiana, Take 2/Last Night/Red Hot Jam/
I'm Worried/I Held My Baby Last Night/Madison Blues/I Can't Hold Out/I Need Your Love/I
Got the Blues

3-70   *Blues Jam in Chicago, Vol. 2*—Blue Horizon 4805
(A)
Worlds in a Tangle/Talk With You/Like It This
Way/Someday Soon Baby/Hungry Country
Girl/Black Jack Blues/Everyday I Have the
Blues/Rockin' Boogie/Sugar Mama Homework

4-70   *Fleetwood Mac in Chicago*—Blue Horizon 3801
(A)/Blue Horizon 66227 (E)
(combination of two above LPs)
(This LP repackaged 1975 as Sire 3715)

9-70   *Kiln House*—Reprise 1004 (E)/Reprise 6408 (A)
This is the Rock/Station Man/Blood on the
Floor/Hi Ho Silver/Jewel Eyes Judy/Buddy's
Song/Earl Gray/One Together/Tell Me All the
Things You Do/Mission Bell

6-71   *The Original Fleetwood Mac*—CBS 63875 (E)
Drifting/Leaving Town Blues/Watch Out/A Fool
No More/Mean Old Fireman/Can't Afford to Do
It/Fleetwood Mac/Worried Dream/Love That
Woman/Allow Me One More Show/First Train
Home/Rambling Pony No. 2
(This LP includes previously unissued 1968–69
tracks)
(American reissue—1977 on Sire Records (A) SR
6045

10-71   *Greatest Hits*—CBS 69011 (E) (compilation)
The Green Manalishi/Oh Well pts. 1 & 2/Shake
Your Moneymaker/Need Your Love So Bad/
Rattlesnake Shake/Dragonfly/Black Magic
Woman/Albatross/Man of the World/Stop Messin' Round/Love That Burns

11-71   *Future Games*—Reprise 6465 (E&A)
Woman of 1000 Years/Morning Rain/What a
Shame/Future Games/Sands of Time/Sometimes/Lay It All Down/Show Me a Smile

2-72   Black Magic Woman—Epic 30632 (A)
            (Repackage of first two American LPs)

3-72   *Bare Trees*—Reprise 2080 (E&A)
            Child of Mine/The Ghost/Homeward Bound/
            Sunny Side of Heaven/Bare Trees/Sentimental
            Lady/Danny's Chant/Spare Me a Little of Your
            Love/Dust/Thoughts on a Grey Day

3-73   *Penguin*—Reprise 2138 (E&A)
            Remember Me/Bright Fire/Dissatisfied/I'm a
            Road Runner/The Derelict/Revelation/Did You
            Ever Love Me/Night Watch/Caught in the Rain

10-73   *Mystery to Me*—Reprise 2158 (E&A)
            Emerald Eyes/Believe Me/Just Crazy Love/
            Hypnotized/Forever/Keep On Going/The City/
            Miles Away/Somebody/The Way I Feel/For
            Your Love/Why

3-74   *Fleetwood Mac/English Rose*—Epic 33740 (A)
            (repackage of first two American LPs)

9-74   *Heroes Are Hard to Find*—Reprise 2196 (E&A)
            Heroes are Hard to Find/Coming Home/Angel/
            Bermuda Triangle/Come a Little Bit Closer/
            She's Changing Me/Bad Loser/Silver Heels/
            Prove Your Love/Born Enchanter/Safe Harbor

3-75   *Vintage Years*—Sire 3706-2 (A) (compilation)
            Black Magic Woman/Coming Home/Rambling
            Pony/Something Inside of Me/Dust My Broom/
            The Sun is Shining/Albatross/Just the Blues/
            Evening Boogie/The Big Boat/Jigsaw Puzzle
            Blues/I've Lost My Baby/Doctor Brown/Need
            Your Love So Bad/Looking for Somebody/Need
            Your Love Tonight/Shake Your Moneymaker/
            Man of the World/Stop Messin' Round/Rollin'
            Man/Love That Burns/If You Be My Baby/Lazy
            Poker Blues/Trying So Hard to Forget

7-75   *Fleetwood Mac*—Reprise 2225 (E&A)
            Monday Morning/Warm Ways/Blue Letter/
            Rhiannon/Over My Head/Crystal/Say You
            Love Me/Landslide/World Turning Sugar
            Daddy/I'm So Afraid

2-77/*Rumours*—Warner Bros. 3010 (A)
Second Hand News/Dreams/Never Going Back Again/

Don't Stop/Go Your Own Way/Songbird/The Chain/You Make Loving Fun/I Don't Want to Know/Oh Daddy/Gold Dust Woman

Bootleg albums

> *Merely a Portmanteau*—TAKRL 1906 (A)
> Rattlesnake Shake/Underway/Tiger/The Green Manalishi/Station Man/Tell Me All the Things You Do

Solo Projects

JEREMY SPENCER
2-70   *Jeremy Spencer*—Reprise 9002 (E)
       Linda/The Shape I'm In/Mean Blues (sic)/String-a-long/Here Comes Charlie (with his Dancing Shoes On)/Teenage Love Affair/Jenny Lee/Don't Go, Please Stay/You Made a Hit/Take a Look Around Mrs. Brown/Surfin' Girl/If I Could Swim the Mountain

3-72   *Jeremy Spencer and the Children*—Columbia 31990 (A)
       Can You Hear the Song/The World in Her Heart/Joan of Arc/The Prophet/When I Looked to See the Sunshine/Let's Get on the Ball/Someone Told Me/Beauty for Ashes/War Horse/I Believe in Jesus

PETER GREEN
6-71   Heavy Heart/No Way Out—Reprise 14092 (E)

1970   *The End of the Game*—Reprise 6436 (A)/Reprise (E)
       Bottoms Up/Timeless Time/Descending Scale/Burnt Foot/Hidden Depth/The End of the Game

(by Peter Green & Nigel Watson)

4-72   Beasts of Burden/Uganda Woman—Reprise 14141 (E)

DANNY KIRWAN
6-75   *Second Chapter*—DJM 454 (E)/DJM DJLPA-1 (A)
       Ram Jam City/Odds and Ends/Hot Summer's

Day/Mary Jane/Skip a Dee Do/Love Can
Always Bring You Happiness/Second Chapter/
Lovely Days/Falling in Love With You/Silver
Streams/Best Girl in the World/Cascades

1976   Ram Jam City/Hot Summer's Day—DJM 1004
        (A)

1976   Man of the World/Best Girl in the World—DJM
        1007 (A)

1977   *Danny Kirwan* (U.S.); in England, *Midnight in
        San Juan*—DJM Records DJL PA-9
        I Can Tell/Life Machine/Midnight in San Juan/
        Let It Be/Angel's Delight/Windy Autumn Day/
        Misty River/Rolling Hills/I Can't Let You Go/
        Look Around You/Castaway

BOB WELCH
(With Paris:)

1-76   *Paris*—Capitol ST-11464 (A)
        Religion/Black Book/Starcage/Beautiful
        Youth/Nazarene/Narrow Gate (La Porte
        Etroite)/Solitaire/Breathless/Rock of Ages/Red
        Rain

8-76   *Big Town, 2061*—Capitol ST-11560 (A)
        Blue Robin/Big Towne, 2061/Pale Horse, Pale
        Rider/New Orleans/Outlaw Game/Money
        Love/Heart of Stone/Slave Trader/1 in 10/
        Janie

11-76   *Big Towne, 2061/Blue Robin*—Capitol 4356

As a solo:

9-77   *French Kiss*—Capitol ST-11663(A)
        Sentimental Lady/Easy To Fall/Hot Love—Cold
        World/Mystery Train/Lose My Heart/Outskirts/
        Ebony Eyes/Lose Your... /Carolene/Dancin'
        Eyes/Danchiva/Lose Your Heart

10-77   *Sentimental Lady/Hot Love—Cold World*—Cap-
        itol 4479

1-78   *Ebony Eyes/Outskirts*—Capitol 4543

Guest Appearances

3-68   **Eddie Boyd with Peter Green's Fleetwood Mac—**

7936 South Rhodes—Blue Horizon 63202 (E)
You Got to Reap/Just the Blues/She's Real/Back
Slack Be Careful/Ten to One/The Blues is Here
to Stay/You Are My Love/Third Degree/Thank
You Baby/She's Gone/(I Can't Stop) Loving
You

4-69   Otis Spann—*The Biggest Thing Since Colos-
          sus*—Blue Horizon 63217 (E)/Blue Horizon 4802
          (A)
          (Peter Green, Danny Kirwan, John McVie) My
          Love Depends on You/Walkin'/It Was a Big
          Thing/Temperature is Rising/Dig You/No More
          Doggin'/Ain't Nobody's Business/She Needs
          Some Loving/I Need Some Air/Someday Baby

5-70   Hungry Country Girl/Walkin'—Blue Horizon·304
          (A)

Related

TRAMP

Tramp was a part-time London blues aggregation. Personnel on first LP included Danny Kirwan, Jo-Ann Kelly,
Dave Kelly, Bob Hall, Bob Brunning, Mick Fleetwood. On
the second, it was Mick Fleetwood, Danny Kirwan, Dave
Brooks, Dave Kelly, Jo-Ann Kelly, Bob Brunning, Bob Hall,
and Ian Morton.

1969   *Tramp*—Music Man 603 (E) (reissued on Spark
          2001 (E))

1974   *Put a Record On*—Spark 112 (E)

CLIFFORD DAVIS

Davis was Fleetwood Mac's manager. He also released two
45's backed by the group. Both sides of the second one
were written by Peter Green.

1970   Come On Down and Follow Me/Homework—Re-
          prise 27008 (E)

1970   **Man of the World/Before the Beginning—
          Warner 14282 (E)/Reprise 27003 (E)**

CREDITS

BOOK COVER PHOTOS Sam Emerson

ALBUM COVER PHOTOS AND ART WORK:

Mr. Wonderful Sire/Blue Horizon Records (P-17)
Kiln House Christine McVie/Warner Bros. Records (P 30, 31)
Bare Trees John McVie (P-41)
The Original Fleetwood Mac Terence Ibbott (P-102)

OTHER PHOTOS

Richard Armas PP-44, 45, 59, 61
Blue Horizon PP-9, 34
CBS/Sire P-20
Glenn Cornick P-46
Sam Emerson PP-4, 44, 45, 46, 48, 54, 58, 59, 60, 61, 62, 64, 67, 69, 70, 74, 77, 79, 82, 87, 88, 103, 104
Nick Easciano P-14
Olivier Ferrand P-103
Eddie Garrick PP-45, 54, 65, 72, 76, 83
Louri Kaye P-45, 46
Paul Canty P-45
Bill Daras Panstenbach PP-54, 58, 60
Neal Preston PP-45, 54, 58, 59, 60, 61
Reprise/Warner Bros. PP-12, 32, 39, 51
Warner Bros. Records P-18
Sharon Weisz PP-28, 44, 46, 47, 54, 58, 59, 60, 80
Judy Wong Private Collection PP-24, 36, 37, 43
Herbert Worthington PP-48, 56, 84, 90
Richard Young PP-47, 60, 103

BOOK DESIGN and ART DIRECTION: Loren Frank

DESIGN CONSULTANT: Brian Flahive

Current Fleetwood Mac Band.

LYRIC REPRINT ACKNOWLEDGEMENTS

BERMUDA TRIANGLE by ROBERT WELCH © 1974 ROCKHOPPER MUSIC (P-99). *BLOOD ON THE FLOOR* by JEREMY SPENCER © 1972 FLEETWOOD MUSIC LIMITED (P-55). *BRIGHT FIRE* by ROBERT WELCH © 1973 FLEETWOOD MUSIC LIMITED (P-88). *CHILD OF MINE* by DANNY KIRWAN © 1972 FLEETWOOD MUSIC LIMITED (P-68). *CRYSTAL* by STEVIE NICKS © 1973 DONA MARTA MUSIC, BUCKINGHAM-NICKS MUSIC & POGO LOGO MUSIC (P-130). *DREAMS* by STEVIE NICKS © GENTOO MUSIC, INC. & WELSH WITCH MUSIC (P-148). *DUST* by DANNY KIRWAN © 1972 FLEETWOOD MUSIC LIMITED (P-69). *EMERALD EYES* by ROBERT WELCH © 1973 FLEETWOOD MUSIC LIMITED (P-92). *GO YOUR OWN WAY* by LINDSEY BUCKINGHAM © 1976 GENTOO MUSIC, INC. & NOW SOUNDS MUSIC (P-147). *THE GREEN MANALISHI (WITH THE TWO PRONG CROWN)* by PETER A. GREEN © 1970 FLEETWOOD MUSIC LIMITED (P-42). *HYPNOTIZED* by ROBERT WELCH © 1973 FLEETWOOD MUSIC LIMITED (P-92). *MAN OF THE WORLD* by PETER A. GREEN © 1970 FLEETWOOD MUSIC LIMITED (P-35). *MILES AWAY* by ROBERT WELCH © 1973 FLEETWOOD MUSIC LIMITED (P-92). *NEVER GOING BACK* by LINDSEY BUCKINGHAM © 1977 GENTOO MUSIC, INC. & NOW SOUNDS MUSIC (P-148). *OVER MY HEAD* by CHRISTINE McVIE © 1975 GENTOO MUSIC, INC. (P-7). *OH WELL* by PETER A. GREEN © 1969 FLEETWOOD MUSIC LIMITED (P-40). *REVELATION* BY ROBERT WELCH © 1973 FLEETWOOD MUSIC LIMITED (P-88). *RHIANNON* by STEVIE NICKS © 1975 GENTOO MUSIC, INC. (P-133). *SECOND HAND NEWS* by LINDSEY BUCKINGHAM © 1977 GENTOO MUSIC, INC. & NOW SOUNDS MUSIC (P-148). *SENTIMENTAL LADY* by ROBERT WELCH © 1972 FLEETWOOD MUSIC LIMITED (P-66). *SHOW BIZ BLUES* by PETER A. GREEN © 1969 FLEETWOOD MUSIC LIMITED (P-39). *SILVER SPRINGS* by STEVIE NICKS © 1976 GENTOO MUSIC, INC. & WELSH WITCH MUSIC (P-148). *TRYING SO HARD TO FORGET* by PETER A. GREEN and C.G. ADAMS © 1978 FLEETWOOD MUSIC LIMITED (P-27).

All Rights Reserved with respect to each of the above copyrights.